GARDEN CARPENTRY

SPAN - ROOF   GREENHOUSE
TOOL SHED : WHEELBARROW
GATES   :   GARDEN   LIGHTS
SUMMER   HOUSE   :   SHELTER
ETC.

British Library Cataloguing-in-Publication Data
A catalogue record for this book is available from the
British Library

Woodworking

Woodworking is the process of making items from wood. Along with stone, mud and animal parts, wood was one of the first materials worked by early humans. There are incredibly early examples of woodwork, evidenced in Mousterian stone tools used by Neanderthal man, which demonstrate our affinity with the wooden medium. In fact, the very development of civilisation is linked to the advancement of increasingly greater degrees of skill in working with these materials.

Examples of Bronze Age wood-carving include tree trunks worked into coffins from northern Germany and Denmark and wooden folding-chairs. The site of Fellbach-Schmieden in Germany has provided fine examples of wooden animal statues from the Iron Age. Woodworking is depicted in many ancient Egyptian drawings, and a considerable amount of ancient Egyptian furniture (such as stools, chairs, tables, beds, chests) has been preserved in tombs. The inner coffins found in the tombs were also made of wood. The metal used by the Egyptians for woodworking tools was originally copper and eventually, after 2000 BC, bronze - as ironworking was unknown until much later. Historically, woodworkers relied upon the woods native to their region, until transportation and trade innovations made more exotic woods available to the craftsman.

Today, often as a contemporary artistic and 'craft' medium, wood is used both in traditional and modern styles; an excellent material for delicate as well as forceful artworks. Wood is used in forms of sculpture, trade, and decoration including chip carving, wood burning, and marquetry, offering a fascination, beauty, and complexity in the grain that often shows even when the medium is painted. It is in some ways easier to shape than harder substances, but an artist or craftsman must develop specific skills to carve it properly. 'Wood carving' is really an entire genre itself, and involves cutting wood generally with a knife in one hand, or a chisel by two hands - or, with one hand on a chisel and one hand on a mallet. The phrase may also refer to the finished product, from individual sculptures to hand-worked mouldings composing part of a tracery.

The making of sculpture in wood has been extremely widely practiced but survives much less well than the other main materials such as stone and bronze, as it is vulnerable to decay, insect damage, and fire. It therefore forms an important hidden element in the arts and crafts history of many cultures. Outdoor wood sculptures do not last long in most parts of the world, so we have little idea how the totem pole tradition developed. Many of the most important sculptures of China and Japan in particular are in wood, and the great majority of African sculptures and that of Oceania also use this medium. There are various forms of carving which can be utilised; 'chip carving' (a style of carving in which knives or chisels are used to remove small chips of the material), 'relief carving' (where figures are carved in a flat panel of wood), 'Scandinavian flat-plane' (where figures are carved in large flat planes, created primarily using a carving knife - and rarely rounded or sanded afterwards) and 'whittling' (simply carving shapes using just a knife). Each of these techniques will need slightly varying tools, but broadly speaking, a specialised 'carving knife' is essential, alongside a 'gouge' (a tool with a curved cutting edge used in a variety of forms and sizes for carving hollows, rounds and sweeping curves), a 'chisel' and a 'coping saw' (a small saw, used to cut off chunks of wood at once).

Wood turning is another common form of woodworking, used to create wooden objects on a lathe. Woodturning differs from most other forms of woodworking in that the wood is moving while a stationary tool is used to cut and shape it. There are two distinct methods of turning wood: 'spindle turning' and 'bowl' or 'faceplate turning'. Their key difference is in the orientation of the wood grain, relative to the axis of the lathe. This variation in orientation changes the tools and techniques used. In spindle turning, the grain runs lengthways along the lathe bed, as if a log was mounted in the lathe. Grain is thus always perpendicular to the direction of rotation under the tool. In bowl turning, the grain runs at right angles to the axis, as if a plank were mounted across the chuck. When a bowl blank rotates, the angle that the grain makes with the cutting tool continually changes between the easy cuts of lengthways and downwards across the grain to two places per rotation where the tool is cutting across the grain and even upwards across it. This varying grain angle limits some of the tools that may be used and requires additional skill in order to cope with it.

The origin of woodturning dates to around 1300 BC when the Egyptians first developed a two-person lathe. One person would turn the wood with a rope while the other used a sharp tool to cut shapes in the wood. The Romans improved the Egyptian design with the addition of a turning bow. Early bow lathes were also developed and used in Germany, France and Britain. In the Middle Ages a pedal replaced hand-operated turning, freeing both the craftsman's hands to hold the woodturning tools. The pedal was usually connected to a pole, often a straight-grained sapling. The system today is called the 'spring pole' lathe. Alternatively, a two-person lathe, called a 'great lathe', allowed a piece to turn continuously (like today's power lathes). A master would cut the wood while an apprentice turned the crank.

As an interesting aside, the term 'bodger' stems from pole lathe turners who used to make chair legs and spindles. A bodger would typically purchase all the trees on a plot of land, set up camp on the plot, and then fell the trees and turn the wood. The spindles and legs that were produced were sold in bulk, for pence per dozen. The bodger's job was considered unfinished because he only made component parts. The term now describes a person who leaves a job unfinished, or does it badly. This could not be more different from perceptions of modern carpentry; a highly skilled trade in which work involves the construction of buildings, ships, timber bridges and concrete framework. The word 'carpenter' is the English rendering of the Old French word *carpentier* (later, *charpentier*) which is derived from the Latin *carpentrius;* '(maker) of a carriage.' Carpenters traditionally worked with natural wood and did the rougher work such as framing, but today many other materials are also used and sometimes the finer trades of cabinet-making and furniture building are considered carpentry.

As is evident from this brief historical and practical overview of woodwork, it is an incredibly varied and exciting genre of arts and crafts; an ancient tradition still relevant in the modern day. Woodworkers range from hobbyists, individuals operating from the home environment, to artisan professionals with specialist workshops, and eventually large-scale factory operations. We hope the reader is inspired by this book to create some woodwork of their own.

WHAT THIS
BOOK IS
ABOUT . .

Gardening and carpentry go very much together. Nearly all the structures and appliances, etc. needed in the garden are made of wood, and in these days of shortages it is invaluable to be able to make your own. Even though you do not make them all yourself it is useful to know how they are made so that you know how to carry out repairs properly.

There are certain obvious items that belong to the subject : greenhouse, lights, shed, barrow, and so on. All these appear in these pages. There are, however, some things for out of doors which many men wish to make but which scarcely come under the heading of garden carpentry. Examples are : trailer caravan, sidecar, canoe, dinghy, henhouse, trek cart, duckhouse, garage, etc., and for these the reader should see the companion volume OUTDOOR WOOD-WORK, published at the same price. It gives designs also for a lean-to greenhouse, portable workshop, standard beehive, cycle stand, kennel, entrance gates, and so on. Details of other WOODWORKER handbooks will be found on the inside cover of this book.

CONTENTS

GARDEN CARPENTRY

SPAN-ROOF
GREENHOUSE, 10 FT. by 6 FT.

THE construction of a span-roof greenhouse of the type usually favoured by amateur gardeners is not a difficult undertaking. The house described is built in sections, which makes for greater strength and has the advantage that the structure can be easily assem_ bled and taken apart.

Throughout the construction an endeavour has been made to specify material of standard size which is normally easily procurable. The precise dimensions of the house are largely determined by these sizes. For instance, it is intended that 21 oz. horticultural glass 24 ins. by 12 ins. should be used, and the exact length of the roof frames is found by allowing 1 ft. 0⅛ in. between the bars plus the widths of the roof timbers. The width of each roof frame

ends, allowance should be made in their lengths for the thickness of these ends, also the inch hang-over of the roof frames. The bars should be positioned similarly to those of the top frames, the side ventilator openings being arranged accordingly. The members of each frame are tenoned together, open mortise and tenon joints being used at the corners.

Referring to Fig. 2, it will be seen that the centre rails are bevelled slightly, and it is necessary to cut the shoulders of the lower tenons to suit this bevel. Some of the members are ploughed to take the glass. Care should be taken to position the grooves so that they agree with the rebates on the bars. Before assembling each frame ½ in. holes for the securing bolts should be bored in the positions

SPAN-ROOF GREENHOUSE BUILT IN SECTIONS. SIZE (AS SHOWN) 10 FT. BY 6 FT.
Dimensions may be modified as required. Height to eaves is 5 ft. Ridge height 7 ft. 6 ins.

is ascertained in a similar way, but in this case ⅛ in. should be allowed for the overlap of the glass panes and 1 in. where the lower panes overlap each bottom rail.

The nominal sizes of the timbers are given, but if prepared stuff is obtained (which is to be preferred) it will, of course, be slightly less in size. The roof frames when in position should overhang the gable ends by 1 in. Before commencing construction it is advisable to determine the precise size of the roof frames as the other sections are dependent on these dimensions.

Side Frames (Fig. 1).—As these butt against the gable

indicated on the drawings. The joints are put together with thick white lead paint and secured with dowels where indicated. Finally each frame should be given a coat of red lead priming.

Gable Ends (Fig. 3).—The pitch of the end frames may be found by setting out on two rods a length corresponding to the width of a roof frame, plus half the thickness of the ridge plate. The two rods are then nailed together with a cross member equal in length to the estimated width of the gable end. The rods when put together will have the form of a triangle. The position of the eaves should correspond with the height of the side frames. Similar joints

1

SPAN-ROOF GREENHOUSE
CONSTRUCTIONAL DETAILS

(See Fig. 10 on next page)

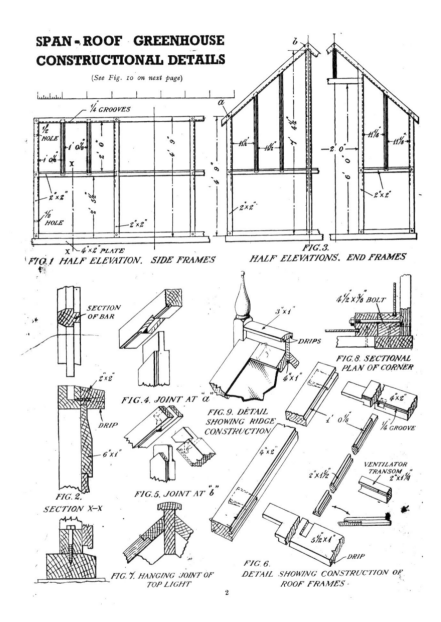

FIG.1 HALF ELEVATION. SIDE FRAMES

FIG.3.
HALF ELEVATIONS. END FRAMES

SECTION OF BAR

FIG.4. JOINT AT "a"

FIG.8. SECTIONAL PLAN OF CORNER

FIG.9. DETAIL SHOWING RIDGE CONSTRUCTION

FIG.2.
SECTION X–X

FIG.5. JOINT AT "b"

FIG.7. HANGING JOINT OF TOP LIGHT

FIG 6.
DETAIL SHOWING CONSTRUCTION OF ROOF FRAMES

2

KEEP YOUR GREENHOUSE WELL PAINTED

are employed to those described in connection with the side frames.

Certain of the members comprising each frame require to be ploughed for the glass. The position of the plough grooves are indicated by dotted lines in the drawings. Figs. 4 and 5 show the joints at eaves and ridge respectively. Before finally securing the joints it is advisable to lay one frame on the other to see that they agree. Each frame is put together in a similar manner to that already described. As before, each completed frame should be given a coat of red lead priming.

Roof Frames (Fig. 6).—The top rails are secured to the stiles by mortise and tenon joints, the tenons being wedged. When cutting the shoulders of the tenons allowance should be made for the rebates on the stiles. It is usual to chamfer the top rails and stiles to agree with the chamfer on the bars, but this complicates the joints and is not necessary. The top rails are ploughed for the glass and the stiles rebated.

The bottom rail of each frame is secured to its respective stiles by bare-faced mortise and tenon joints. The mortises are slightly below the rebates; thus, when the glass is in place it will be slightly above the surface of each bottom rail. This provides a space whereby the moisture collecting on the interior of the glass can find exit. The underside of each bottom rail is ploughed close to its outside edge to provide a drip. It is also advisable to provide similar grooves on the underside of each stile where it projects from the gable end.

The edge of the top rail is bevelled so as to fit closely to the ridge plate. The bottom ends of the bars are housed into bottom rail. The form of joint shown prevents any moisture getting into the joint and causing rot. Care should be taken to see that the rebates are level with those on the stiles. The transoms for the top ventilators are scribed to the bars and secured in position by oval nails.

Side and Top Ventilators.—The construction of the ventilators is not illustrated as the joints employed are similar to those used for securing the top rails to the stiles in the roof frames. Moulded stuff of suitable section for the side ventilators can be obtained, but as the top ventilators require to be 1¼ ins. thick only, the material will have to be specially prepared. The top ventilators are duplicates in miniature of the roof frames, but in this case there is no need to provide condensation spaces. The hanging joint is shown in Fig. 7. This arrangement is effective in preventing water reaching the interior of the house via the joint.

Door (Fig. 10).—The design of the door shown is probably the best for a greenhouse, but if the worker finds that it is beyond his capabilities, a plain ledged and braced door formed from matching will do quite well.

Erection.—It is advisable to rest the house on a 4 ins. by 2 ins. plate so that the lower members of the house are clear of the ground. The plate is halved together and treated with creosote. In order to prevent any possible subsidence, each corner should rest on bricks, or a concrete slab, let into the ground. Care should be taken to see that the bricks or concrete are level. When the plate is laid down, a gable end can be placed in position and secured to the plate by coach bolts. A side frame is then rested on the plate in its correct position and the holes for the fixing bolts continued through the end already in position. The two frames can then be bolted together. The side frame is also secured to the plate by coach bolts.

A similar procedure is followed in connection with the erection of the other sides. When the sides are assembled the corner battens can be nailed in place, their position being shown in Fig. 8. The sills are bevelled at a similar angle to that of the middle rail of each side frame and rebated to take the ship-lap boarding. Reference to Fig. 2

will make this clear. The sills are mitred at corners and particular care should be taken to see that the joints are well painted. It is advisable to screw the sills in place. In nailing the weather boarding it is necessary that the nails should be driven into the framing so that it is possible at any future time to take the house apart.

It is necessary to remove the apex of each gable end so that a flat surface is provided on which the ridge plate can rest. As shown in Fig. 9 the ends of this member are flush with the gable ends. When one roof section is in position the ridge plate is nailed to this section and the other roof section is brought into position so that it abuts against the ridge. Both roof sections are secured to the gable ends by screws so as to be removable. At this stage the finials can be fixed, each finial being accommodated in a slot cut in the roof frames. The capping is cut so as to fit tightly between the finials and is nailed to the ridge plate. White lead paint should be freely applied to all joining surfaces.

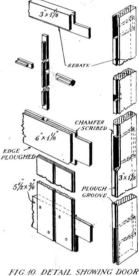

FIG. 10. DETAIL SHOWING DOOR CONSTRUCTION

Glazing.—In order to secure the glass it is only necessary to embed the panes in putty. Top putty does not serve any useful purpose but has a disadvantage inasmuch that it tends to crack, and the rain settling in the cracks will in time cause the timbers to rot. Each pane is made secure by panel pins.

Gutter.—It is advisable to provide the house with a gutter; otherwise the surrounding earth will become saturated with water to the detriment of the house. The gutter shown comprises two 4 ins. by ¾ in. battens nailed together to form a V. Each length of gutter is supported by brackets, each bracket having a V-shaped notch in which the gutter rests. The gutters should be arranged so as to have a slight fall. As the gutter at the end opposite the door has to drain into the side gutter, the end gutter will have to be positioned above the side gutter and be provided with a hole so that the water will flow into the side gutter and then by way of an extension to a water butt.

Painting.—The outside and inside of the house should be given two coats of white lead paint, and further coats at yearly intervals. A pleasing appearance can be obtained by giving the ship-lap boarding a coat of green paint.

SUMMER HOUSE
FOR THE SMALL GARDEN

A QUIET RETREAT.

The Summer house is octagonal in form, with a width (over all) of 7 feet. The height to apex (excluding finial) is 10 ft. 3 ins.

HERE is an attractive garden shelter, suitable alike for children or for the old folks. The favourite octagonal shape has been adopted and the first step is to set out the plan in full size.

This may be done on the floor of a spare room. Fig. 10 shows the method. Chalk out a square of 7 ft., squaring the corners by measuring the diagonals which are also chalked. With a lath about 4 ft. long and a couple of nails draw the circle indicated, this having a diameter of 7 ft. Complete the octagon by chalking in the remaining four sides, these of course being parallel to the diagonals. Test the length of each side ; then mark a template by nailing eight strips of wood together. Brace them with cross pieces to keep all angles correct.

A concrete foundation (Fig. 4) will be advisable. Failing this, bricks laid header and stretcher-ways under each of the eight angles will serve.

Timber.—Sound red deal is suitable for the purpose, using weatherboards for roof and sides, and tongued and grooved 1 in. boards for floor.

The house is sectional, with eight side frames, the roof, and the floor ; hence construction can be carried on in the workshop. All the side frames are equal in length and width, five of them (A, B, C, D, and E) being as shown in Fig. 1. The two frames (F and H) on each side of the door opening will have lower cross rails 36 ins. high (Fig. 2). The door frame (G) has of course no cross rail and the top and bottom rails will be the same thickness as the posts.

Side Frames.—Those shown in Fig. 1 have the rails set back the thickness of the weatherboards, say, about ¾ in., to allow the boards to come flush with the posts (Fig. 6). The same applies to the bottom rails of frames (F and H). All frames are mortised and tenoned together, the tenons being taken right through. Use thick paint

when assembling and pin the joints with oak dowels. Shoot all edges straight and true and then bevel off to the correct angle for meeting (Fig. 1, section).

Erect the frames on the site prepared, using handscrews to hold them together. The frames can be bolted together, or, alternatively, screwed and braced with galvanised angle irons (Fig. 1). If bolted, then three bolts to each joint should be enough. Drill the holes and put the bolts in before nailing on the weatherboards. For convenience, the nailing on of the weatherboards can be left until the roof is ready to go on.

Roof and Rafters.—Prepare wall plates (Fig. 5), half lapping them together at the angles to form a frame to sit on top of the sides. The outside edges of the frame should be about flush with the sides (Fig. 4). The finial (Fig. 3) must be of tough hardwood such as oak or teak, and is from 6 in. square stuff. Cut and plane it to the octagonal shape, taper the top, and shape or turn the bottom end. Sink mortises in all faces for the roof rafters, which are tenoned to it somewhat in the manner of an open umbrella. The plan of the complete roof frame is shown in Fig. 8.

The rafters are notched over the wall plates (Fig. 5), cutting off a bit of the corner for the purpose. All the rafters are uniform in size, and the length determines the pitch of the roof.

A weatherboard covering is most effective, but the roof could be boarded with ¾ in. match-boarding and covered with zinc or felt if desired, slips being nailed over the joints.

The weatherboards to the sides (Fig. 9) may be vertical as indicated in Fig. 4, or, alternatively, horizontal. Fillets are nailed down each post (Fig. 1) to form rebates for nailing.

Decorative bracing pieces might be introduced over the door and window openings as shown in the perspective sketch, or windows could be fitted as indicated in Fig. 2. A removable door would also be valuable for

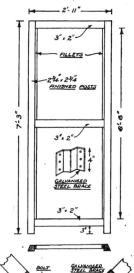

FIG. I. ELEVATION OF SIDE FRAMES.

4

THE SIDE SECTIONS ARE BOLTED TOGETHER

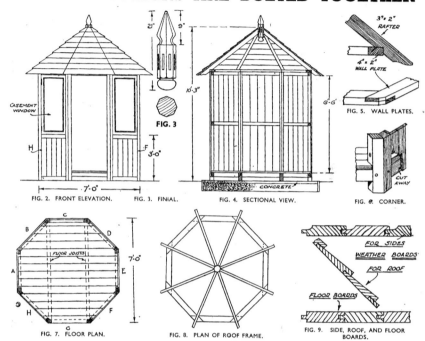

FIG. 2. FRONT ELEVATION.   FIG. 3. FINIAL.   FIG. 4. SECTIONAL VIEW.   FIG. 6. CORNER.

FIG. 3   FIG. 5. WALL PLATES.

FIG. 7. FLOOR PLAN.   FIG. 8. PLAN OF ROOF FRAME.   FIG. 9. SIDE, ROOF, AND FLOOR BOARDS.

use in bad weather and to protect the interior through the winter months.

The Floor.—Should be of stout boards out of 1-inch stuff, properly planed, tongued and grooved (Fig. 9). It rests upon the bottom rails of the side framing and on a couple of joists across the centre (Fig. 7). The boards are notched round the posts and, to facilitate possible subsequent removal, could be screwed to the rails instead of nailing. The fixed seat (if required) should be placed upon bearers screwed to posts.

The timber list is as follows :—

						ft. ins.	ins.	ins.
16 Posts	.	.	.	.	.	7 3	$2\frac{3}{4}$	$2\frac{3}{4}$
6 Rails	.	.	.	.	.	2 11	3	$2\frac{1}{2}$
17 Rails	.	.	.	.	.	2 11	3	2
2 Joists	.	.	.	.	.	6 6$\frac{1}{2}$	6	2
8 Wall plates	.	.	.	.	4 0	4	2
8 Rafters	.	.	.	.	.	5 3	3	2
1 Finial	.	.	.	.	.	1 9	$5\frac{1}{4}$	$5\frac{1}{4}$

Approximately 200 feet of tongued and grooved weatherboard for the sides in 25 lengths at 7 ft. long and 10 lengths at 2 ft. 6 ins! long at 6 ins. wide by $\frac{3}{4}$ in. thick

Approximately 160 feet run of weatherboard or matchboarding for roof at 6 ins. wide by $\frac{3}{4}$ in.

About 80 feet run of planed, tongued and grooved floor boards at 6 ins. wide by $\frac{7}{8}$ in.

A saw to be used for outdoor woodwork should generally have more set than one used for furniture making. This is chiefly because the timber is often damp, and a saw with small clearance is inclined to jam. In any case keep a rag soaked in oil handy and wipe over the blade occasionally. It will also be useful to ease the working of such tools as the plane.

If you are tackling a piece of outdoor woodwork for the first time

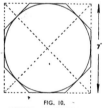

FIG. 10.
METHOD OF SETTING OUT THE OCTAGONAL PLAN TO 7 FEET.

you will find a tendency to become careless with your tools. You bring them out in a bag, and you soon find yourself flinging them in in a heap as you finish with them. Avoid it as far as you can. Tools jarring across each other soon lose their edge and the quality of your work deteriorates.

5

GARDEN SEAT

IN making a garden seat, always aim at rigidity. Do not stint the thickness. You sit out of doors to relax, and the greater your sense of security the better you understand what complete abandonment to effortless relaxation really means. Aim, too, at comfort, provision for which can be made under three general heads : (1) A height at which you may sit at ease ; (2) a front-to-back depth of seat which will afford adequate rest for the legs ; and (3) a rake which will support the body without throwing it too far back. There must, of course, be variation (within limits) according to height and build of sitter, but in the seat shown the average has been considered. Height of seat is 15 ins., tilting to 14½ ins. at back. (This will allow for light cushions.) Depth of seat is 20 ins. from front to line of lower back rail. Rake of back is 2½ ins., this being arranged without involving waste in cutting shaped back legs.

The cost of timber for a garden seat is not unduly heavy even if oak is selected. Failing this, there is larch, although (if available at present) the red Baltic pine, commonly known as red deal, will serve admirably if kept well painted. The length of seat shown is 4 ft. 6 ins., but it may be anything from 4 ft. to 5 ft., always bearing in mind that the larger size is more economical in the long run.

Ends.—Front legs are 2½ ins. square ; back legs 3 ins. by 2 ins. The reason for this latter size is that the back legs may be kept straight, the rake being effected by the placing of the back rails. Front legs are chamfered on the two front edges, the upper part being stop-chamfered also on the back edges. All legs are mortised for the seat rails and stretcher rails, noting that the seat at back is ½ in. lower than at front. The front legs have ⅝ in. stub tenons to enter the arms (see Fig. 3). Back legs, tapered and shaped at top, are mortised for back rails and either mortised or notched for arms. When assembling the ends, fit the joints with red lead paint (thick). Cramp up well.

(Continued on opposite page)

FIG. I. ORNAMENTAL AS WELL AS USEFUL.

Oak or teak are first choice, but larch makes a quite satisfactory alternative. Length 4 ft. 6 ins.

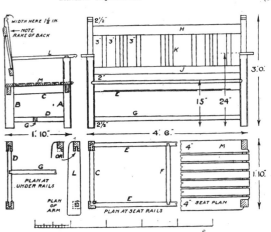

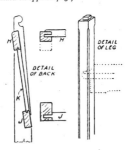

FIG. 3. HOW PROVISION IS MADE FOR SLOPING BACK. ALSO DETAILS OF FRONT LEG.

FIG. 2 (left). SCALE WORKING DRAWINGS, END AND FRONT ELEVATIONS, PLANS, ETC.

LAWN TABLE

THE light garden table shown here was made entirely from oddments of oak, no piece of which exceeds 3 ins. in width. The size over top (shown 27 ins. by 18 ins. in the diagram) may be varied as required, whilst the height may be anything from 26 ins. to 30 ins. according to the average height of garden seat used. The parts required for a table of the dimensions indicated are :

		Long	Wide	Thick
		ft. ins.	ins.	ins.
(A)	4 Legs	2 10	2	$\frac{5}{8}$
(B)	2 Battens	1 6	3	$\frac{1}{4}$
(C)	Rail	2 1	2	$\frac{3}{4}$
(D)	9 Laths	2 3	$1\frac{3}{4}$	$\frac{3}{8}$

If the height of table is lessened, keep the width across legs at ground equal to the width of top. Keep the width over legs at top 3 ins. less than that at ground.

The legs are halved where they intersect. If a full size set-out is made on the back of a waste sheet of wallpaper,

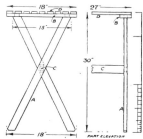

FIG. 2. ELEVATIONS WITH MAIN SIZES.

FIG. I. A TABLE THAT YOU WILL FIND HANDY IN THE SUMMER
Main sizes are 30 ins. high, 27 ins. long, and 18 ins. deep.

the halving joint, the top tenons, and the ground line are readily ascertained. The legs are tenoned to the battens and are held midway by the stretcher rail (C) which is tenoned right through and wedged at each end. Plot the mortise carefully so that it does not cut away the halving unduly. The shoulders can be very wide. Joints are fixed with paint.

The number of top laths (D) used may be determined by the width of stuff available, but from $1\frac{3}{4}$ ins. to $1\frac{1}{4}$ ins. gives the best effect. The spaces between are about $\frac{1}{8}$ in., and the laths are fixed with brass screws well countersunk in.

If only required for light purposes the table is a very simple one to make, and if to be painted or varnished can be carried out in softwood.

GARDEN SEAT

(*Continued from opposite page*)

Assembling.—Prepare the back, carefully spacing for the splats (K) which are tongued to rails (H and J). Note that splats are flush with rails on face. Turning to Fig. 3, observe that, whilst the lower rail (J) is kept flush with front face of back legs, the upper rail (H) is thrown towards the rear face—this to provide for the rake. Adjust the mortises accordingly. The lower rail (J) will have a shouldered tenon ; the upper one (H) a barefaced tenon so that the back of rail slightly overlaps the leg.

With the long seat rails (E) ready, assemble the seat. The cross rail (F) and the long stretcher (G) may be dovetail housed. Should the worker prefer front and back underframe rails instead of the single stretcher, these may be tenoned to legs, raising the rails an inch or more so that the tenons clear those of rails (D). Peg the tenons. Again see that all joints are well painted. Test the piece for squareness and cramp up.

Arms are $4\frac{1}{4}$ ins. wide at front and $3\frac{3}{4}$ ins. or 4 ins. at back. At back they are either tenoned or notched to leg ; at front they overhang the leg by 2 ins. (shaping as indicated) and are held by stub-tenoning and pegging. Round the corners front and back and take the arris off upper and under edges.

For the seating it is wise to ·use 4 ins. wide boards at front and back, rounding the edges over at end. All boards slightly overhang the seat rails (C). Screw down, countersinking well for the heads.

If to be painted, give a priming of red lead, followed by at least two coats of oil paint. If a preservative such as creosote is preferred give three dressings.

CUTTING LIST

			Long	Wide	Thick
			ft. ins.	ins.	ins.
(A)	2 Front legs		2 0	$2\frac{1}{2}$	$2\frac{1}{2}$
(B)	2 Back legs		3 0	3	2
(C)	2 Seat rails		1 10	$2\frac{1}{2}$	$1\frac{1}{4}$
(D)	2 Stretcher rails		1 9	$1\frac{7}{8}$	$1\frac{1}{2}$
(E)	2 Seat rails		4 6	$2\frac{1}{2}$	$1\frac{1}{4}$
(F)	Cross seat rail		1 9	$2\frac{1}{2}$	$1\frac{1}{4}$
(G)	Stretcher		4 5	$1\frac{7}{8}$	$1\frac{1}{2}$
(H)	Top back rail		4 6	3	$1\frac{1}{4}$
(J)	Lower back rail		4 6	$2\frac{1}{2}$	$1\frac{1}{4}$
(K)	10 Splats		1 0	$1\frac{1}{4}$	$\frac{5}{8}$
(L)	2 Arms		2 0	$4\frac{1}{4}$	$1\frac{1}{4}$
(M)	2 Seat laths		4 6	4	$\frac{7}{8}$
	5 do.		4 6	$2\frac{1}{4}$	$\frac{7}{8}$

Lengths allow for joints and fitting. Thicknesses are net.

7

FIG. I. HANDY FOR THE MOWER, TOOLS, AND ODDMENTS.
A size of 5 ft. 6 ins. by 4 ft. is generally useful. The erection is not costly and will accommodate mower, roller, etc. The shed shown here can be dismantled.

W HEN building a shed the size must be suited to individual requirements. Thus any design given can be only in the nature of a suggestion. As alternatives to wood for the roof and sides asbestos-cement sheet (also obtained corrugated for roofs) and corrugated iron might be considered.

TOOL SHED

It is desirable for several reasons that the shed should be easily dismantled. Thus the four sides will be made as separate frames bolted together. The roof, span or flat (sloping), will be a separate unit, whilst the floor will be nailed down. A portable shed is usually provided with a concrete foundation which preserves it from ground moisture. Or, in another way, the corners might stand on small brick piers. If to be a fixture the outer posts of front and back frames are often cut about 24 ins. longer, charred and sunk into the ground.

So far as size is concerned a minimum is about 5 ft. 6 ins. by 4 ft. over the frames (before boarding). Anything smaller hardly repays cost and labour. Height is necessarily determined by normal stature. If a door of 6 ft. is allowed the head room inside will be ample. At this height obviously a more pleasing proportion for the shed is procured if the plan dimensions are increased, but this incurs more timber. A span roof, not acute, is indicated ; but, if preferred, a boarded and battened plain roof may be substituted, this sloping gently (say, 6 ins. to 8 ins.) to the back. It will overhang a few inches.

End Frames (Fig. 2).—Taking the end frames, the front (door) frame is erected as at Fig. 2. Stuff 2 ins. by 2 ins. should be ample if the timber is sound, but if the shed is increased in size heavier stuff is desirable. In most cases halving joints will serve, but the bottom rail (B) should be tenoned to the outer posts (see Fig. 4). The span roof joints will also be clear from Fig. 4, pieces C and F are halved to pieces B and C and notched to F. At the apex these latter are nailed to the ridge pieces (G). All joints should be painted with thick paint before nailing.

The back frame is similar in size to front frame, but does not require the inner posts (D). Thus, instead of the

(Continued on page 11.)

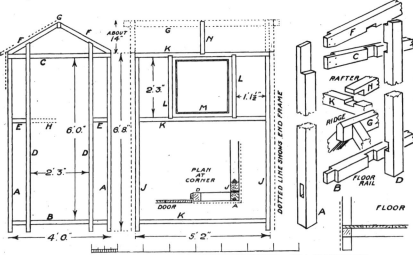

FIG. 2. FRONT FRAME TO SCALE.   FIG. 3. SIDE FRAME SHOWING WINDOW.   FIG. 4. THE JOINTS USED.

TRELLIS SCREEN

WITH a little touch of shrubbery for a background, a screen of this type can be wonderfully attractive. Although creeper can be grown upon it this is not necessary in cases where shrubs abound. The size shown is a convenient average; but, as any modification entails no change as far as the actual construction is concerned, height and length may be adjusted according to the size of the garden and the space available.

Timber.—The ground space occupied is 6 ft. by 2 ft. 8 ins., and the screen is built in three sections, bolted together. In this way it is convenient for removal at any time. In ordering timber for the posts remember to allow an extra 12 ins. or 15 ins. for sinking into the ground.

If Western red cedar is available it is the favourite timber for such a purpose. Otherwise, red deal may be used. All joints, tenoned and halved, will be fitted with *paint.* Remember too that, when timbers overlap, the meeting parts should be smeared with paint. Whatever timber is used, the ends which enter the ground must be well tarred.

Back.—This, for stability, is given two posts at each end. These may finish 2 ins. square for a screen of the height. Mark each outer part (A) for the mortises to take the three main rails (B, C, and D), also for the intermediate thinner rails (F). Note from the enlarged detail section that the main rails (B, C, D) are $1\frac{3}{8}$ ins. wide (or they might be only $1\frac{1}{8}$ ins.), finishing flush at back to allow for the upright bars (G) which are nailed on in front.

The intermediate rails (F) may finish $1\frac{1}{8}$ ins. by $\frac{7}{8}$ in., being tenoned to the posts so that their faces are in alignment with faces of rails (B, C, and D) to serve as bearers for the upright (G). These latter are spaced as shown and nailed on. It will be understood that the rails (B, C, D) run right across to the outer posts (A), being halved to the intermediate posts (E).

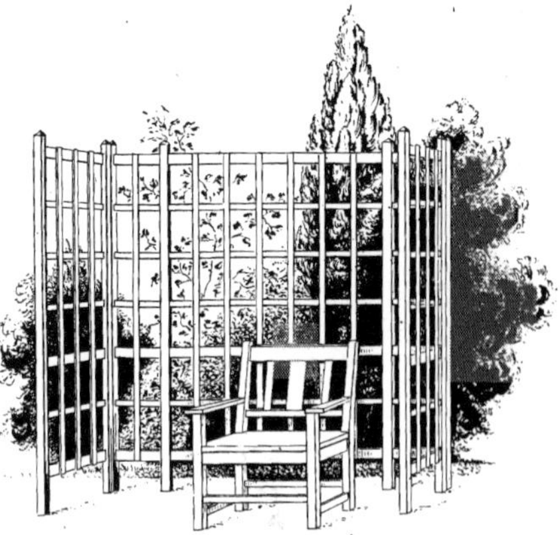

FIG. 1. GARDEN SCREEN. HEIGHT 6 FT.
Plan size, 6 ft. by 2 ft. 8 ins., or may be adapted.

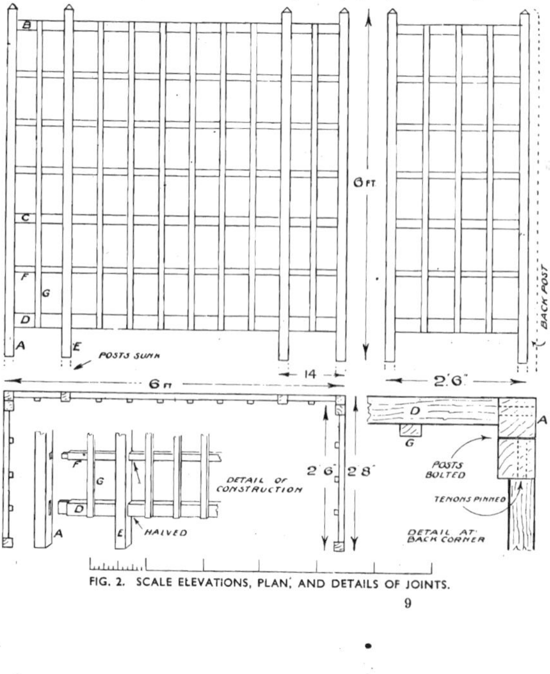

FIG. 2. SCALE ELEVATIONS, PLAN, AND DETAILS OF JOINTS.

The ends.—These are made in the same way as the back, except that there are no intermediate posts. They are secured to the back by bolts.

	ft.	ins.	ins.	ins.
(A) 6 Posts .	7	3	2	2
(B) 1 Rail .	6		2	$1\frac{1}{8}$ or $1\frac{3}{8}$
2 Rails (Ends)	2	6	2	$1\frac{1}{8}$ or $1\frac{3}{8}$
(C) 1 Rail .	6	0	2	$1\frac{1}{8}$ or $1\frac{3}{8}$
2 Rails (Ends)	2	6	6	$1\frac{1}{8}$ or $1\frac{3}{8}$
(D) 1 Rail .	6	0	3	$1\frac{1}{8}$ or $1\frac{3}{8}$
2 Rails (Ends)	2	6	3	$1\frac{1}{8}$ or $1\frac{3}{8}$
(E) 2 Posts .	7	3	2	2
(F) 4 Rails .	6	0	$1\frac{1}{8}$	$\frac{7}{8}$
8 Rails (Ends)	2	6	$1\frac{1}{8}$	$\frac{7}{8}$
(G) 14 Uprights	5	4	$1\frac{1}{8}$	$\frac{5}{8}$

Lengths allow for fitting. Widths and thicknesses are net.

When you paint woodwork pay special attention to the end grain, because this is the most vulnerable part of the wood. Remember, too, that end grain is essentially porous so that the paint, especially the first priming coat, is liable to be soaked up. It is, therefore, advisable to give such parts an extra coat of priming. It is largely owing to its protective quality that paint is used for assembling outdoor woodwork. It holds the parts without being affected by the damp, and, in the event of the latter penetrating, it keeps it out of the end grain necessarily exposed at the joint.

GARDEN OR SEASIDE SHELTER

THE shelter indicated measures 6 ft. by 4 ft. on plan, the height at the back 5 ft. 9 ins. In addition a canopy extension 6 ft. long is shown. This is especially useful if the shelter is made as a bathing tent as it may be lowered completely to enclose the front.

Posts.—The folding framework (Fig. 2) consists of two front uprights 6 ft. 3 ins. long, and two back uprights 5 ft. 9 ins. long. All the uprights should be of hardwood, at least 1¼ ins. square, and 1 in. metal ferrules are fitted to top ends as in Fig. 3. It is also necessary to fit a stout

slat are pivoted together with a small iron rivet and washers, as in Fig. 5.

The two complete slats are pivoted together in the centre in the same way, and are attached to the uprights with screws and washers as in Fig. 6, the pivoting points being given in Fig. 4.

End Slats.—The slats at the two ends are arranged as in Fig. 7. Each slat has a total length of 5 ft. 5 ins. centre to centre, the lower portion being 4 ft. 7 ins., and the top portion 10 ins. centre to centre. Rivets and washers are

FIG. I. EASILY ERECTED SHELTER WHICH WILL GO INTO THE CAR.

This provides a screen from wind and sun without excluding fresh air. Plan size is 6 ft. by 4 ft. Height (front) 6 ft. 3 ins., (back) 5 ft. 9 ins. The whole thing folds into a roll 6 ft. 3 ins. long, plus the spikes.

spike at the end, this being easily contrived by driving in a fair size wire nail and removing the head.

Slats.—The uprights are connected at sides and back by thin wood pivoted slats arranged in such a way that they allow the uprights to be folded but keep them firm when extended. The slats connecting the two back uprights are arranged as in Fig. 4. Good straight-grained hardwood should be used for slats as they must bear the strain of being pivoted together with rivets. They are attached to uprights with screws and washers. Stuff 1⅛ ins. by ⅜ in. should be sufficient if suitable wood is used.

Each of the two slats is in two portions. The total length centre to centre is 7 ft., the lower and longer portion being 5 ft. 4½ ins. long, centre to centre. The top portion is 1 ft. 7½ ins. centre to centre. The two portions of each

again used to pivot the portions of the slats together, and the slats are attached to the uprights as before. Care should be taken to see that the pivoted joints work quite freely. Washers, besides being used under the heads of the rivets and screws, could also be placed between the joints.

Top Rods.—The extended framework is joined at the top with front, back, and side top rods as in Fig. 2. These rods should also be of hardwood, those for the front and back being 5 ft. 9½ ins., and for the sides 3 ft. 9½ ins. long by 1 in. diameter. Ferrules are fitted to the ends of the rods and screw eyes bored into them (Fig. 8). The screw eyes enable the rods to be fitted over the spikes at the ends of the uprights.

Canopy.—If a front extension canopy is fitted, two

10

AN INVALUABLE ITEM FOR THE SUMMER MONTHS

uprights must be arranged to support it. The uprights should be 6 ft. 3 ins. long by 1¼ ins. diameter, and ferrules and spikes should be fitted at both ends as in Fig. 9. A top rod is provided to join the two canopy uprights and two other rods join the canopy uprights and the front uprights to the shelter.

To secure the canopy extension it will be necessary to fit guy ropes to the two uprights. The ropes should have a metal thimble spliced or tied to the top end, as at Fig. 10. A peg (Fig. 11) shaped from a piece of stuff 10 ins. long by 1¼ ins. wide by ¾ in. thick, is used to secure each guy rope to the ground, and from the peg the end of the rope is brought up to a wood toggle (Fig. 12) shaped from another piece of stuff 4 ins. long by 1 in. wide by ½ in. thick.

Two holes are bored in the toggle, one threaded over the guy rope, the end of the rope being passed through the other and knotted. The toggle is slid up or down the rope to tighten or loosen it. On completion the framework should receive a coat of varnish.

Canvas.—As good a quality tent canvas as can be afforded should be used to cover the shelter. The sheet covering the back and side is made as one. Fairly wide hems should be run round the edges for strength, and if eyelet holes are worked in the top hem as shown in Fig 13 they may be used to hang the sheet on the spikes at the top ends of the uprights.

Strong tapes should be sewn between for tying to the top rods, and tapes at the front edges are used for tying to the front uprights. The roof of the shelter and the canopy could be in one piece with a valance about 4 ins. deep sewn around the edges. Eyelet holes are worked to pass over the spikes at the ends of the uprights. Small turned wood finials (Fig. 14) could be provided to fit over the spikes on the uprights to give a pleasing finish.

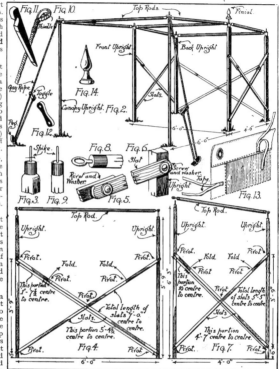

FIGS. 2 TO 14. GARDEN SHELTER : DIMENSIONS AND DETAILS OF CONSTRUCTION.

TOOL SHED

(Continued from page 8)

fillings (E), a mid bar (dotted line H, Fig. 2) will be carried across to support the boarding.

Side Frames (Fig. 3).—These, note, are intended to be bolted *within* the end frames. Thus the length is given as 5 ft. 2 ins. (not 5 ft. 6 ins.). They are put together in the same way as end frames, rails (K) tenoned or halved to posts (J). In one side provision should be made for a window (size as desired). This can be done by notching in the two uprights (L) and making a separate window frame (M) which could be hinged to the top bar. A mid rafter (or two if thought necessary) will be fitted as at N. Allow the ridge (G) to overhang about 3 ins. at each end.

Boarding.—If tongued and grooved stuff is available

¾ in. will do. Boarding of 4 ins. or 4½ ins. looks better than 6 ins. If the roof is to be covered with waterproof felting ⅜ in. will also serve here. Flooring, however, should be ⅞ in., and, whether fixed lengthwise or across, a mid joist should be fitted. It will be seen that, as the flooring rests on bottom bars (B and K), it is raised about 5 ins. from ground. The boarded door will be ledged and braced, using ⅞-in. boards and 1¼-in. battens.

A ground plan of 5 ft. 6 ins. by 4 ft. does not permit of much elasticity in the way of inside fittings. There should, however, be ample space for shelves. A small bench, it may be added, is exceedingly useful, and if the window were fitted at the back with top about 27 ins. by 15 ins. would be possible. A height of 3 ft. is handy. If the shed is to be used for housing a lawn mower or roller, a sloping platform for easy travel is usually provided.

11

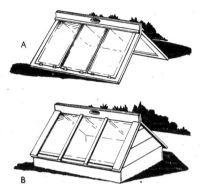

A

B

FIG. 1. TWO INVALUABLE GARDEN ITEMS.

Any number of the cloches shown at A can be placed together end to end. Both these and the frames B can be folded flat when not in use.

GARDEN LIGHTS AND CLOCHES

AUTUMN, winter, and spring are the seasons when cloches and lights may be put to the greatest use in the garden. A cloche is shown at A (Fig. 1), and a frame at B. They are probably the most convenient form of cloche and light yet designed, being inexpensive, adaptable to any requirements, and made to fold for transport or storing. The length may be extended by placing a number of lights end to end.

A section through a frame is shown in Fig. 2, and the method of making the lights in Figs. 3 and 4. The lights may have the glass fitted loose, and held with a fillet at the top and metal clips at the bottom, or it may be rebated in and puttied. Dimensions could be arranged to suit individual needs, and to meet any special sizes of glass available. In the drawings each light is 4 ft. long by 1 ft. 9 ins. wide. The top rail in Fig. 3 is 4 ft. long by 6 ins. deep by 1 in. thick, bottom rail 4 ft. long by 4 ins. wide by 1 in. thick, stiles 1 ft. 9 ins. long by 4 ins. wide by 1 in. thick, and muntins 1 ft. 9 ins. long by 2 ins. wide by 1 in. thick. The bottom edge of the top rail is planed to an angle of 45 degrees, and all the members are half-lapped and screwed together. Semi-circular weather grooves are cut near the edges of the stiles and muntins as shown. The loose fitting glass is held by a fillet about ⅜ in. wide by ⅜ in. thick fixed to the top rail, and two metal clips are fixed to the bottom rail to hold each pane of glass.

Some adjustments of sizes are necessary in the members of the frame (Fig. 4) in which the glass is to be fixed with putty. The top rail is 4 ft. long by 6 ins. deep by 1 in. thick, bottom rail 4 ft. long by 4 ins. wide by ⅞ in. thick, stiles 1 ft. 9 ins. long by 4 ins. wide by 1¼ ins. thick, and muntins 1 ft. 9 ins. long by 2 ins. wide by 1¼ ins. thick. The stiles are rebated ⅜ in. square on their inner top edges, the muntins are rebated on both top edges, and a groove

is cut in the top rail to receive the glass. Mortise and tenon joints fixed with screws are again used for framing. The lights should be hinged together as shown in Fig. 2, and a long hook made from stout wire or small iron should be fitted across two opposite muntins to hold the lights open. It will also be found a convenience if hand-holes are cut in the top rails.

The frame in Fig. 5 may be made up from any light boards about 6 ins. wide. The ends are 2 ft. 4 ins. wide by 1 ft. 9 ins. high in the centre and 8 ins. at the sides, battens about 1½ ins. wide being nailed around the edges. The sides are 3 ft. 10 ins. long by 8 ins. wide, with light battens nailed a short distance in from the ends. The parts of the frame may be fixed together by driving screws at the corners, or hooks and eyes could be arranged as shown in Fig. 6.

All screws to be used in exposed positions should be dipped into vaseline or grease to protect them from rust. In the case of oak, brass screws are advisable owing to the strong acid in the wood which is liable to cause corrosion. This will probably result in blue stains appearing on the surface. If iron screws *must* be used be generous with the vaseline, and make sure that the screw head is painted. Brass screws should not be driven directly into hard oak as they may break off. Put in an iron screw first, and replace with brass afterwards.

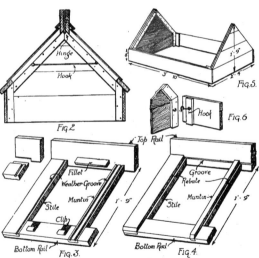

FIG. 2. PRINCIPAL SIZES AND DETAILS OF CONSTRUCTION

SECTIONAL RABBIT HUTCHES

T HESE hutches enable rabbits to be kept under the best possible conditions, and, although a start may be made with a single hutch, further sections may be added as the stock increases. Many odd pieces of wood may be worked in; wood obtained from packing cases is especially suitable, and the idea of working in short lengths has been borne in mind. Three sections are required for a start—a hutch, base, and roof section—to which other hutch sections may be added as required.

Fig. 1 shows three hutch sections surmounted by a roof section, and standing on a base. Details of all three sections with the dimensions are shown in Fig. 2. The wood used should be about 1 in. thick. A start will probably be made on the hutch section, and the front frame put in hand first.

Hutch.—The frame is shown in Fig. 3, and is made with pieces of 2 in. wide stuff, half-lapped and screwed together. Openings for two doors have to be arranged, that on the right enclosing the sleeping compartment, and that on the left the day run. The body of the hutch is made with two ends built up from short lengths of wood and cross-battened, as in Fig. 4. To these the boards forming the back and bottom are nailed (see Fig. 2). The back finishes level with the top

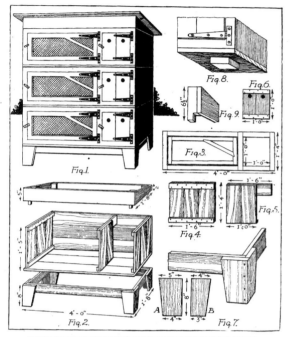

Fig.1.

Fig.2.

Fig.3.

Fig.4.

Fig.5.

Fig.6.

Fig.7.

Fig.8.

Fig.9.

A B

A STYLE OF HUTCH WHICH WILL HELP YOUR FOOD PRODUCTION EFFORT.
The great advantage of this design is that you can start off with one hutch only and add to it as the necessity arises. Actual use has showed them to be successful.

and bottom edges of the ends, and the bottom is wide enough to enable it to be nailed to the edges of the back and the front frame. The latter is fixed to the front edges of the ends, and a division (see Fig. 5) is made up and fixed inside the hutch to divide the day and night compartments.

A solid wood door (Fig. 6), battened on the inside and provided with two ventilation holes, encloses the night compartment, and a framed door of 2 in. wide stuff, half-lapped and screwed together, encloses the day compartment. It is advisable to fit a strut across this door frame to prevent it from dropping, and wire netting is nailed on the inside. Both doors are hinged on the right-hand side, and fitted with turn-buttons or other means of fastening.

Base.—The base section is made with four angular pattern legs joined by four cross rails, details being shown in Fig. 7. For each leg two pieces of 1 in. stuff (A and B) are required. The wider piece is nailed to the narrower, and the cross rails are nailed or screwed inside.

Roof.—The roof section is made with two ends 1 ft. 6 ins. long by 5 ins. wide at the front and 2 ins. wide at the back. A front 5 ins. wide and back 2 ins. wide are nailed to them, and blocks of wood 6½ ins. long by 2 ins. wide by

1 in. thick are nailed in the corners, while the roof is formed with boards arranged to give ample overhang at all sides. An outer covering of roofing material should be tacked around the edges.

In fitting the sections together, blocks should be nailed under the four corners of the hutch section as shown in Fig. 8. They are kept about 2 ins. in from the end and 1 in. in at the front and back to enable them to drop down in the opening of the base section. To fit the roof section to the hutch, the projecting ends of the corner blocks are cut in about 1 in. from the end edges, as shown in Fig. 9, to allow the roof section to drop down on to the hutch.

In any outdoor structure avoid relying entirely upon screws or nails if possible. It is much better to cut a notch or some other simple joint, because the notch itself resists any tendency for the wood to shift. The nails serve rather to prevent the wood from leaving the notch. Another point is that it makes for accuracy. If the notch is truly marked out the work must be accurate, whereas there is room for considerable error when nails only are used. In fact the hammer may knock the work out of truth, especially if the nails are entered askew.

13

GARDEN WORKSHED
PORTABLE SHED, EASILY DISMANTLED

ALTHOUGH a concrete foundation is an advantage, in the case of a temporary structure it will be sufficient to remove the turf and lay three deals, or planks, about 7 ins. by 3 ins. running lengthwise of the shed, at the front, back and middle. The foundation for the deals should be small piers of brick or concrete, three to each deal. It will be advisable to make a portable floor in three sections, and the deals form a good seating for the floor joists, which should be 4 ins. by 3 ins. if it is intended for a workshop. Otherwise 3 ins. by 3 ins. will be satisfactory. An alternative is to form

AN ATTRACTIVE DESIGN THAT WOULD ENHANCE A GARDEN.
Length 9 ft., width 7 ft. Height to eaves 6 ft. 6 ins.

a concrete base, about 8 ins. wide, in place of the deals. In this case it should go all round with a strip down the middle to support the joists.

All the framing consists of 3 ins. by 2 ins. with novelty sidings for the boarding as shown in the illustrations. The span roof is covered with western red cedar shingles. The sections consist of back, two ends, and two front frames; the roof is in two parts for easy transport. If the shed is made of larger dimensions than those shown, it is better to construct the back in two sections as in Fig. 3. Also the sashes would be better divided and the middle post of the front frames carried through.

End Frames.—These are 2 ins. thick and put together with halving joints. They consist of three posts, three horizontal rails, and inclined rails to the pitch of the roof at the top, as in Fig. 1. A piece is fixed to the top rails to provide a seating for the ridge, and it also serves as a fixing for the centre post. It should project at least 1 in. on the inside. The sidings are cut flush with the side posts, and 3 ins. by 1 in. strips are planted to cover the ends of the boards both on the ends and sides.

The back framing is 3 ins. thick as in Fig. 3, and presents no difficulties. It consists of four posts and three rails, all halved together where they cross each other. The rails are housed into the corner posts and the posts are housed into the top rail.

Front Frames.—The front consists of two separate frames, 3 ins. thick, one on each side of the door as in Fig. 2. The joints are housed, except for the intersection between the middle post and bottom rail which is a halving joint. It is necessary to secure the feet of the door posts with metal dowels about 2½ ins. by ½ in. These will be let into the supports whether of concrete or

wood. If the glass in the sashes is too large to suit the worker a vertical bar may be included, or the middle post run through and four small sashes used instead of the two large ones. Fig. 6 shows the detail for the sill and the arrangement for the bottom rail of the sash. If the rebate on the sill is planted, 1½ in. stuff will be satisfactory. The details for the door post are given in Fig. 7, which shows a planted stop for the door, also serving as a cover for the ends of the sidings. It is also necessary to plant pieces on the posts at the sides of the sashes,

between the sill and the siding above the sash. All the vertical framing can be prepared on the ground with the sidings nailed in position, or the frames may be boarded when erected.

Assembling.—The separate pieces of framing should be erected and nailed together temporarily, so that the nails can be easily withdrawn, and the holes bored for the bolts (B). It is better to use square-headed bolts. Snap heads have a better appearance, but if corrosion takes place it is a difficult matter to remove the nuts; with square heads spanners can be used on both head and nut. If the heads are considered unsightly they can be sunk into the framing and covered by the sidings, and they are just as effective. Two or three ⅜ in. bolts should be used at each corner, and it is advisable to use washers, especially under the nuts. The bolt holes should be large enough to allow for easy removal of the bolts.

Roof.—When the framing is erected bolt the eaves plates along the front and back framing as in Fig. 8. The positions of the bolts are shown in plan, Fig. 3. It is necessary to use two bolts to each of the front frames, but three bolts are sufficient at the back. If the back is made in two sections as shown by the alternative detail in Fig. 3 four bolts should be used. Bolt the two ridge pieces together and place them in position. Then nail the rafters securely to the eaves plate and ridge taking care that the nails do not fix the separate pieces together. If the work is done carefully the rafters, plate, and ridge for each side should be rigid, and easily lifted off when the bolts are removed. The two middle rafters should have collars bolted to them to prevent the door posts from being thrust outwards.

(Continued on page 17)

14

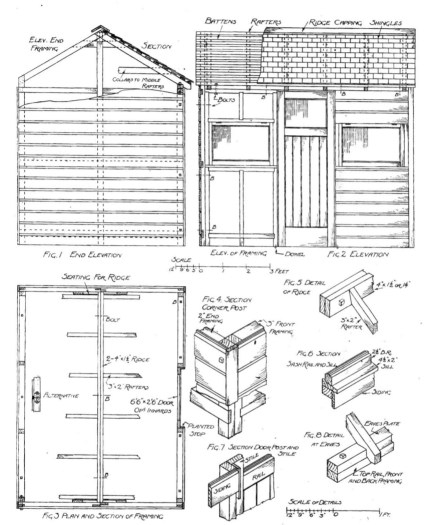

ELEV. END FRAMING   SECTION

COLLARS TO MIDDLE RAFTERS

FIG. 1 END ELEVATION

BATTENS   RAFTERS   RIDGE CAPPING   SHINGLES

BOLTS

ELEV. OF FRAMING   DOWEL   FIG. 2 ELEVATION

SCALE
12 9 6 3 0   1   2   3 FEET

SEATING FOR RIDGE

BOLT

2-4"×1½" RIDGE

3"×2" RAFTERS

ALTERNATIVE

B

6'6"×2'6" DOOR OPS INWARDS

FIG. 3 PLAN AND SECTION OF FRAMING

FIG. 4. SECTION CORNER POST
2" END FRAMING   3" FRONT FRAMING

PLANTED STOP

FIG. 7. SECTION DOOR POST AND STILE
STILE
SIDING   RAIL

FIG. 5 DETAIL OF RIDGE
4"×1½" OR 1¼"
3"×2" RAFTER

FIG. 6 SECTION
SASH RAIL AND SILL
2½" D.R.
4½"×2" SILL
SIDING

EAVES PLATE
FIG. 8 DETAIL AT EAVES
TOP RAIL, FRONT AND BACK FRAMING

SCALE OF DETAILS
12" 9" 6" 3" 0   1 FT.

SCALE ELEVATIONS AND GENERAL DETAILS OF CONSTRUCTION

15

GARDEN FRAMES

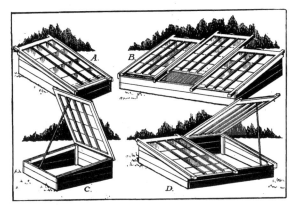

FIG. 1. TWO TYPES OF FRAMES IN VARIOUS SIZES

Both sliding and hinged types are equally satisfactory. Size can suit personal requirements. See Figs. 2-11 on opposite page.

THERE are two types of garden frames—those with sliding lights, and those with hinged lights. Although there is little to choose between them the sliding type is, perhaps, favoured by the professional gardener, but single or even double-hinged light frames are satisfactory and are preferred by many amateurs.

In the choosing, some consideration should be given to the position the frame will occupy. It should of course face south, but if there is a wall or fence at the back (which will naturally give added protection), then the hinged type is certainly the best because a hinged light may be opened for ventilation where a sliding light cannot. It is probably the question of space which causes the amateur to favour the hinged light.

Types.—Fig. 1 (A) shows a single frame with a sliding light; (B) a frame with three sliding lights; (C) a single frame with hinged light; and (D) a double frame with hinged lights. Almost any kind of wood 1 in. thick may be used for the frames, but deal of course is most easily worked. Fig. 2 shows a frame for two sliding lights, and from its description it will be simple to make a single or three-light frame.

The standard size adopted for lights is mostly 4 ft. wide by 6 ft. long, but it is not necessary to always use these dimensions. In determining the size of the two-light frame (Fig. 2) the length is calculated by the width of the two lights plus 1 in. the thickness of the middle guide-piece which is fitted between them, while the width of the frame should be arranged to allow 1 in. overhang of the lights at both the front and the back. Thus for two 6 ft. by 4 ft. lights the frame should be 8 ft. 1 in. long by 5 ft. 10 ins. wide at the top. The depth may be from 1·ft. to 1 ft. 6 ins. at the front, and 1 ft. 6 ins. to 2 ft. at the back.

Making the frame.—The two ends (Fig. 3) of the frame should be made first. Boards to make the size and shape are held together with battens nailed 1 in. from the front and back edges. The top ends of the battens should stand ¼ in. below the top edges of the ends, and it will be an advantage if a weather groove is worked along these edges, as shown at Fig. 4.

The front and back of the frame is also made with 1-in. boards which fit between the ends and are nailed to the battens at their edges. To accommodate the double lights a runner 3 ins. wide is carried across the middle of the frame, to which it is lapped and nailed as shown at

Fig. 5. Weather grooves should again be cut in the runner, and a guide-piece 2 ins. deep is nailed above. Battens 3 ins. wide are nailed across the front and back under the runner. Finally, guide-pieces 4 ins. deep are nailed across the ends on the outside to stand 2 ins. above their top edges. From this description it will be simple to arrange for one, two, or three light frames.

Hinged Light Frame.—A frame for a single hinged light is shown in Fig. 6, and it is made with two ends joined by front and back boards as before. Size is arranged by allowing a 1 in. overhang for the light all round. The ends (Fig. 7) are made with boards cut to the required size and held together with battens nailed 1 in. in from the front and back edges, with another batten fitted between these battens and standing down about ¼ in. from the top edges of the ends.

Again it will be advisable to work weather grooves along the top edges (see Fig. 8 for details). The front and back are nailed to the battens on the ends as before, and a hingeing batten is nailed across the top edge of the back. If a double frame is desired, the necessary length is allowed, and a middle batten (or runner) and guides-piece is fitted as in the whole frame for the sliding lights previously described.

Lights.—A light suitable for these frames is shown in Fig. 9, deal 2 ins. thick being used for the making. Top rails hould be 4 ins. wide, stiles 2½ ins. wide for sliding light and 4 ins. for hinged light, bottom rail 4 ins. wide but only 1½ ins. thick, and astragals 1½ ins. wide. The top rail and stiles should be rebated and chamfered ⅛ in. on the inner edges and the astragals on both edges, but the bottom rail is only chamfered on the inner edge, while weather grooves are run on the outer bottom edges, details being shown in the sections in Fig. 10.

The top and bottom rails are tenoned into the stiles, the joints being mitred into the depths of the rebates and chamfers, and the face of the bottom rail is kept level with the rebates to allow the glass to fit over it. The astragals are tenoned into the top rail and run over the bottom rail, where grooves ¼ in. deep are prepared for them, details being shown in Fig. 11. If a frame smaller than 6 ft. by 4 ft. is being made it would be possible to reduce the thickness of the light to 1½ ins. Glazing should be with 21 oz. glass. Two or three coats of paint should be applied.

16

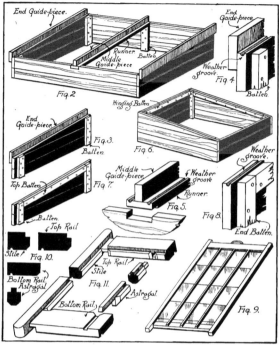

GARDEN BASKET

This is handy for gathering garden produce, and may be made to any convenient size. The sides are of ⅛ in. stuff 18 ins. long by 6 ins. wide. The bottom is a piece of thin plywood nailed to the sides. Two small battens about ¾ in. wide

IDEA FOR GARDEN BASKET.

by ⅛ in. thick are fixed across the ends to strengthen the plywood, and two battens about ¾ in. wide by ⅜ in. thick are fixed across the bottom about 8 ins. apart to form a firm bearing. The handle could be formed from a piece of thin wood which will readily bend, or it may be made as shown in the alternative sketch with two straight upright pieces joined by a piece of dowel rod.

CONSTRUCTION OF THE FRAMES AND THEIR LIGHTS. (See opposite page.)

GARDEN WORKSHED

(Continued from page 14.).

The battens for the shingles should be 3 ins. by 1 in. They should run over the end frames about 2 ins. or 3 ins. The ends may be covered with narrow barge boards to give a more finished appearance. The gauge for the battens should be about 5 ins., as shingles should not have more than 5 ins. margin. The bottom batten should be 1¼ ins. thick to serve as a tilting fillet.

The shingles can now be nailed to the battens taking care to keep them ⅛ in. apart to allow for expansion. The nails should be galvanised, and 1 in. from the edges to avoid splitting the shingles. It is necessary to keep the nails 6 ins. from the butts so that they are covered by the shingle next but one above. This provides an attractive and serviceable roof for the garden and is worth the cost and trouble. It requires about 300 random width shingles, 16 ins. long, for the given roof, or 360 for an area of 100 sq. ft., or one square. Small wood gutters may be fixed to the feet of the rafters, but they are not usual for garden sheds.

Door and Sashes.—Any type of door may be used, but the example shown has a much better appearance than the usual batten door. It is easily made and it is an interesting example of woodworking. The rebate for the glass is continued for the boards below, and the stiles are chamfered through, so there is no difficulty with the shoulders. The boards, or battens, are shown with vee joints. A pair of 4 in. butts are used for hanging the door ; an ordinary rim lock is sufficient for securing the door.

The sashes are made from ordinary 2 ins. by 2 ins. sash stuff with a wider bottom rail, 2½ ins. or 3 ins. They are hinged at the top with 3 in. butts, and require a stay at the bottom for opening. A rebate may be planted round the inside if desired, but it is not necessary. It is advisable to throat the stiles and bottom rail to prevent water working through by capillarity. There is some protection, however, due to their being set back from the face of the sidings.

A shed of this description should be painted on the front and any other portion that is on view from the garden. The back may be creosoted, this being a better protection than paint. The shingles should be left untreated as western red cedar does not require any protection and weathers to a grey colour.

17

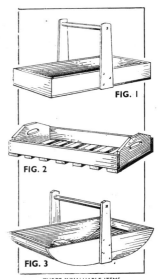

FIG. I

FIG. 2

FIG. 3

THREE INVALUABLE ITEMS.
Fig. I shows the weed box, Fig. 2 the fruit tray,
and Fig. 3 the basket.

WEED BOX, FRUIT TRAY, AND BASKET

Sides may be 3 ins. wide, dipping to 2½ ins. at the middle, as shown in the working diagram, or may be kept straight at a width of 2½ ins. or 2¾ in. Shape the ends as indicated, cutting hand-holes 4½ ins. by 1½ ins. Screw sides to ends (C) and screw or nail on the bottom slats.

Basket (Fig. 3).—Size 20 ins. by 15 ins.

Parts required:—2 Sides, 20 ins. by 5 ins. by ⅜ in. 2 End battens (D), 15 ins. by 2¼ ins. by ⅜ in. Bottom bar (E), 15 ins. by 2¼ ins. by ⅜ in. Bottom (ply), 26 ins. by 15¼ ins. by ¼ in. 2 Handle uprights, 12 ins. by 2¼ ins. by ½ in. Handle bar, 15¼ ins. by 1¼ ins. square.

The framework of this basket consists of the two shaped sides connected by the three battens (D and E). The curves of the sides are obtained by spacing the uprights at 7 ins. as indicated in the working diagram. The outer battens (D) may be very slightly curved on the outer faces to facilitate the nailing on of the plywood bottom. Bottom batten (E) may be let in and screwed to sides ; the end battens are nailed on or screwed.

The thin plywood bottom (F) is cut so that the outer plies run crosswise. In this way it is easily bent to shape. Nail first to the bottom batten (E) ; then bend and nail to each side. When nailing to the outer battens (D) use long wire nails which can be clinched inside. The handle supports with octagonal bar (G) are fixed as described for Fig. 1.

THESE can be made from oddments of wood, and will prove extremely useful.

Weed Box (Fig. 1).—Size, 16 ins. by 10 ins. or 18 ins. by 11½ ins.

Parts required:—2 Sides, 16 ins. by 4 ins. by ½ in. 2 Ends, 10 ins. by 4 ins. by ½ in. or ⅝ in. 2 Handle uprights, 11 ins. by 2⅛ ins. by ½ in. Handle bar, 11½ ins. by 1¼ ins. square. Bottom (ply), 16¼ ins. by 10¼ ins. by ⁷⁄₁₆ in.

Rebate the sides for the ends (A) and screw or nail. Nail on the plywood bottom, driving the nails in wedgewise, and trim the edges. Shape the handle supports, tapering in length from 2⅛ ins. to 1¾ ins., bevel the bottom edges and cut ½ in. square mortises for tenons on handle bar. Screw the uprights in position.

Work the handle to an octagonal section (B), leaving tenons at ends. Wedge the tenons when assembling. It is advisable to paint all joints before screwing or nailing.

Fruit or Vegetable Tray (Fig. 2).—Size, 21 ins. by 13 ins. or may be any size up to 24 ins. by 15 ins.

Parts required:—2 Sides, 21 ins. by 3 ins. by ½ in. 2 Ends 12 ins. by 5½ ins. by ⅝ in. Bottom : 2 pieces 13 ins. by 3 ins. by ½ in., 5 pieces : 13 ins. by 1½ ins. by ½ in.

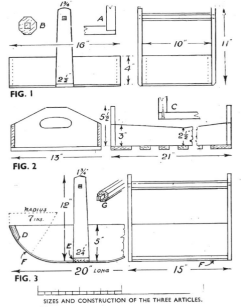

FIG. I

FIG. 2

FIG. 3

SIZES AND CONSTRUCTION OF THE THREE ARTICLES.

GARDEN WHEELBARROW

CONVENTIONAL TYPE

FIG. 1. USEFUL TYPE OF GARDEN WHEELBARROW.
Can be fitted with pneumatic-tyred wheel, or one of wood or metal, whichever is available.

THIS wheelbarrow is shown with a pneumatic wheel which makes a wonderful difference in the ease with which the barrow can be handled. A diameter of 14 ins. for the wheel is recommended. Needless to say, the wheel and accessories should be obtained before any timber is cut.

The usual woods are ash or oak for the shafts and elm for the body and legs. For a cheaper barrow red deal is frequently used for the body parts.

Chassis.—The first step is to make, on a sheet of stiff lining paper, a full-size plan of the chassis (Fig. 4). Draw a centre line 5 ft. long and at the right hand end square off a width of 2 ft. for the spread of the handles. The taper is determined by the length of wheel spindle and must be obtained by testing. Take the wheel and place the spindle boxes in position on the spindles, allowing about $\frac{1}{8}$ in. for play. In this way the spacing of the shafts (A) can be ascertained accurately and the line of shafts drawn in. Mark off for the cross rails (B) and also for the shaped handles.

Cross rails (B) are 3 ins. wide by $1\frac{1}{4}$ ins. thick, tenoned to the shafts. Note, however, that as the barrow floor is flush with the top of shafts (see Fig. 3) a $\frac{3}{4}$ in. shoulder is allowed on the cross rails.

Body.—Assuming that the barrow has a 14 ins. wheel and that the plan approximates that at Fig. 4. the front board (Fig. 5) may be cut to a width of 14 ins. at bottom and 21 ins. across top, the height at centre being $13\frac{1}{2}$ ins.

The barrow back (Fig. 6) can be allowed a width of 20 ins. at bottom, splaying to 26 ins. at top. Height at centre may be $9\frac{1}{2}$ ins.

The sides (see Fig. 2) have the same angle at both ends. In cutting, allow 25 ins. at bottom and 37 ins. at top. Allow a little for final trimming, and fix the height (centre) at 12 ins.

The angles shown in the diagrams will be a sufficient guide for the experienced worker in adjusting his joiner's bevel, as trifling modifications in size do not affect the usefulness of the barrow.

The Floor, with its joints painted, is cut to shape so that it fits exactly up to the splay of the shafts inside, and with its length such that it gets a good bearing upon the cross rails and beds flat down upon them throughout. The body may be put together independently after a trial fit as the work proceeds and be later skew-nailed and screwed to the framework. It is desirable to use brass screws. The body sides are stiffened in their housings by screwing through at each end, and a further stiffening is by means of lengths of screwed fillet 1 in. square introduced into the angle formed by the front projection before trimming as per dotted line, Fig. 2.

The knee pieces (Fig. 7), in pairs, for front and back are cut to the sizes given, the angle again being obtained by means of the joiner's bevel.

The Legs (Fig. 10) are cut from lengths of 26 ins., 4 ins. by $2\frac{1}{2}$ ins. The upper ends (about 9 ins.) are splayed to agree with the angle of sides which they support. They are screwed in position in addition to being slightly notched to the shafts. The brackets which stiffen the legs in position can be cut to shape (Fig. 8) from pieces 12 ins. by 4 ins. so that they project each side of the leg. They are in one piece and can be slightly recessed to fit on the leg and be screwed up to the underside of the shafts. A further stiffening is afforded by means of long bolts and nuts, the length being sufficient to pass right through the shafts at X, Fig. 2, and project about 1 in. each end where they are threaded for a final screwing up with nuts and washers.

Wheel.—In fitting the pneumatic tyred wheel, the spindle boxes (gauged to their proper distance apart) can be screwed direct to the shafts. These boxes are holed on one side, but stopped on the outside so that the spindle revolves with its ends concealed in the box. When spindle boxes are not supplied with the wheels these can be fixed in position by means of bearing blocks (Fig. 9) cut from 2 ins. by $2\frac{3}{4}$ ins. stuff to finish 10 ins. long. Such wheel blocks will be bored for the spindle to pass and project at each end sufficiently to allow the tapped ends of the spindle to be adjusted with nuts and washers.

If deal is used for making the barrow it is essential that it is given a yearly coat of creosote to preserve it. Pay special attention to the end grain.

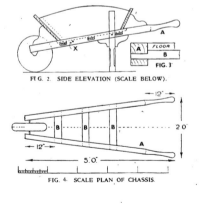

FIG. 2. SIDE ELEVATION (SCALE BELOW).

FIG. 3.

FIG. 4. SCALE PLAN OF CHASSIS.

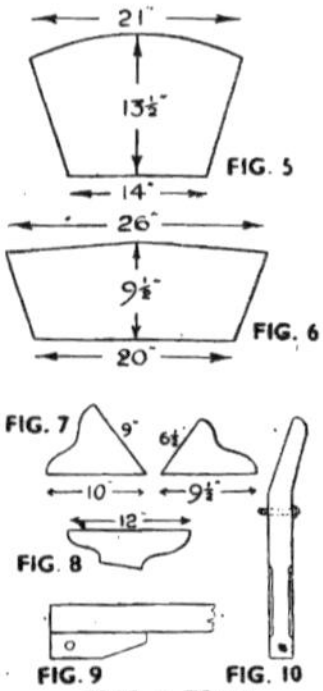

— 21" —
$13\frac{1}{2}$"
— 14" —
FIG. 5

— 26" —
$9\frac{1}{2}$"
— 20" —
FIG. 6

FIG. 7 — 9" — $6\frac{1}{2}$"
— 10" — $9\frac{1}{2}$" —
FIG. 8 — 12" —

FIG. 9   FIG. 10
FIGS. 5 TO 10.

19

CHAIRS AND TABLE FOR THE LAWN

ALL three articles shown here are portable and of light construction. Hardwood is of course essential. For the deck chair ash is the usual wood. Ash or birch would be suitable for the folding armchair, whilst for the table oak, birch, beech, or ash may be taken. Finish may be by staining and varnishing, or by enamelling in a soft colour.

FOLDING ARMCHAIR (Figs. 2-9)

Cross Seat Frames.—Prepare first the two cross-leg frames (Fig 2). The outer of these (Fig. 3) consists of two legs 25 ins. by 1⅛ ins. by ⅝ in. framed into a top rail 17 ins. by 1⅝ ins. by 1 in. A connecting rod (14 ins. by ⅝ in. diam.) is fitted below as shown. The legs are tenoned into the top rail, the rod being simply entered through. Round off all sharp edges and fix with glue and wire nails.

The inner frame (Fig 4) is made in exactly the same way except that, in width, it must fit within the outer frame with ⅛ in. clearance (see A and B, Fig. 7). Pivoting holes of ¼ in. diameter are bored in the positions shown in Figs. 3 and 4, and the frames are pivoted together with ¼ in. iron rivets. Washers ⅛ in. thick are placed between the frames to give a clearance when folding, and washers about $\frac{1}{16}$ in. thick are placed under the heads of the rivets.

Side Frames.—The two side frames (C, Figs. 5 and 7) are made with two legs 27 ins. long by 1⅝ ins. wide by 1 in.; top rail 19 ins. long by 2½ ins. wide by 1 in.; bottom rail 16 ins. long by 2½ ins. wide by ⅝ in.; filling rail 16 ins. long by 4¼ ins. wide by ⅝ in.; and a back extension piece 20 ins. by 1⅝ ins. wide by 1 in.

The bottom rail is tenoned into legs, the legs into top rail, and the filling rail into top and bottom rails. The top rail should project 1 in. beyond back edge of back leg where it is tenoned into the back extension piece (Fig 6). The latter is bevelled off at the bottom to fit against back leg and give a slope to back of seat. All outside edges should be neatly rounded over, the joints being glued and fixed by driving wire nails or wood pins from the edges of the framework, while the lower end of extension piece is screwed or nailed to back leg.

FIG. I. THREE ITEMS THAT CAN BE MADE ALMOST ENTIRELY FROM STRIP MATERIAL.
Folding armchair, deck chair with canopy, and light tea table.

Assembling.—The sides and cross frames are assembled as shown in Fig. 7. The joints at the bottom are pivoted on ¼ in. rivets as before described, the positions for boring the pivot holes being shown in the various illustrations. Special notice should be taken of the circular filling blocks at the bottom of the narrow cross leg frame which are necessary to make up the difference in width between the two frames.

The cross frames are also attached to the leg frames near the top (Fig. 8), with iron stretcher plates (Fig. 9). These plates are 6½ ins. long by ⅝ in. by ⅛ in. in section, ¼ in. Holes are bored as shown, and they are attached with ¼ in. rivets and washers. It will be noticed that one plate of each pair is cranked forward, this being necessary because of the difference in width of the frames. The chair is completed by tacking on a canvas seat and back. The seat should be 16 ins. or 17 ins. wide, and the back 8 ins.

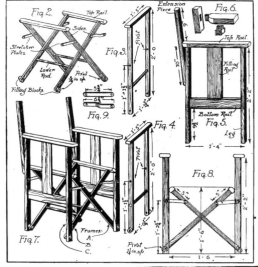

and the bottom rail of frame (Fig. 12) will be required to engage these notches to regulate the height and slope of chair. The bottom edge of this rail should be bevelled as in Fig. 15 before framing the rail.

Assembling.—All the joints should be glued, and may be fixed by driving wire nails through the edges of sides. The three frames (A), (B), and (C) are pivoted together with rivets and washers (see Fig. 17), but the canopy frames (D) and (E) are attached with $\frac{1}{4}$ in. bolts and wing-nuts, as in Fig. 18. The complete assembly is shown in Fig. 19. To finish the chair a length of 1 ft. 6 ins. wide, striped or plain chair canvas is tacked between the top rails of the frames (A) and (B) with sufficient fullness to make a comfortable seat. The canopy is made up from the same material, with sides from 4 ins. to 6 ins. deep.

TEA TABLE (Figs. 20—26).

The Parts.—The legs are about 2 ft. 1 in. long (allowing for the rubber tyred castors) by $1\frac{1}{4}$ ins. square, joined at the top by two side rails 1 ft. 9 ins. by $4\frac{1}{2}$ ins. by $\frac{3}{4}$ in.; two top end rails 1 ft. 4 ins. by $1\frac{1}{2}$ ins. by $\frac{3}{4}$ in.; and two bottom end rails 1 ft. 4 ins. by $1\frac{1}{4}$ ins. by $\frac{1}{2}$ in. In framing the dimensions shown in Figs. 20, 21 and 22 should be observed, the side rails being tenoned into

DECK CHAIR (Figs. 10—19).

Frames.—This chair is made with five frames, lettered A, B, C, D, E. The sizes of these are as follows :—

Frame A (Fig. 10) : two sides 3 ft. $5\frac{1}{2}$ ins. by $1\frac{1}{2}$ ins. by $\frac{7}{8}$ in.; top rail, 19 ins. by 2 ins. by $\frac{7}{8}$ in.; bottom rail, 19 ins. by 1 in. diameter.

Frame B (Fig. 11) : two sides, 4 ft. by $1\frac{1}{2}$ ins. by $\frac{7}{8}$ in.; top rail, 21 ins. by 2 ins. by $\frac{7}{8}$ in.; bottom rail, 21 ins. by 1 in. diameter.

Frame C (Fig. 12) : two sides, 23 ins. by $1\frac{1}{2}$ ins. by $\frac{7}{8}$ in.; bottom rail, 23 ins. by 2 ins. by $\frac{7}{8}$ in.

Frame D (Fig. 13) ; two sides, 22 ins. by $1\frac{1}{2}$ ins. by $\frac{5}{8}$ in.; top rail, $24\frac{1}{2}$ ins. by 1 in. diameter.

Frame E (Fig. 14) : two sides, 10 ins. by $1\frac{1}{4}$ ins. by $\frac{5}{8}$ in.; top rail, 23 ins. by 1 in. diameter.

The wide cross rails are tenoned into the sides, but the round rails are shouldered down to $\frac{3}{4}$ in. diameter and bored in. All edges of the sides should be slightly rounded. Notches are cut in the edges of the sides in frame (Fig. 10) as shown,

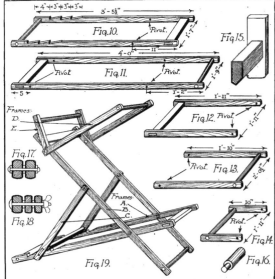

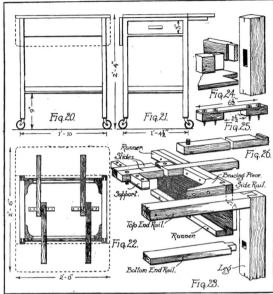

FIGS. 20 to 26. DETAILS OF GARDEN TEA TABLE.

HOW FIELD GATES ARE HINGED

In this matter the practice varies. Almost all village carpenters have their own methods. A 9 ft. or 10 ft. five-barred field gate as Fig. 1 will probably have hanging stiles of 5 ins. by 3 ins. stuff, the shutting stiles being 3 ins. or 4 ins. by 3 ins. If the rails are 3 ins. by 1¼ ins., tenoned to the stiles, they will be thicknessed up at the hanging side (A, Fig. 2) to take the heavy strap hinges which will be about 2 ft. in length. The strap hinges (B) pivot on pins which pass right through the gate posts and are bolted. The hinges are bolted to the gate.

For a gate which is to open either way the pin is bolted as at C—that is, *in line* with the gate. In this case, of course, the gate will not open beyond the right angle unless a greater space is allowed between the post and stile.

For a gate to open inwards and well back, the pin is bolted through the post at an angle (say, 45 degrees) as at D. The angle may be greater if required.

If the gate is to open right back, describing a complete semicircle, the socket of the strap hinge is forged as at E. the angle enabling the gate to clear the post as it swings open.

the legs, the top end rails dovetailed, and the bottom end rails tenoned in as in Fig. 23.

The legs are also joined with four bottom rails, two being 1ft. 9 ins. and two 1 ft. 4 ins. by 1¼ ins. by ½ in. tenoned as in Fig. 24, with a shelf of thin wood fitted below. The top framing is strengthened by fitting bracing pieces 4 ins. by 2 ins. by ¾ in. at the corners. These are dovetailed into side framing rails and screwed to top end rails.

Top.—The table top is of ⅝ in. stuff, the main portion being 2 ft. by 1 ft. 4½ ins., and the flaps 2 ft. by 6¾ ins., hinged on the under side. Two pairs of slides are used to support the flaps, and they are fitted up as in Figs. 22 and 23. Each slide is 1 ft. 3 ins. by 1¼ ins. wide by ¾ in. and slots 1¼ ins. wide by ¾ in. deep are cut in the top edges of side rails of leg framing for them to work through.

Supports.—Two supports are fitted under top for the slides to work in. The supports consist of two blocks 2 ins. by 1 in. by ¾ in. spaced 2½ ins. apart, and joined by a thin metal plate 6½ ins. by 1 in. wide, the whole being fixed under top with four screws as in Fig 25. A wood peg is fitted through the inner end of each slide to prevent its being pulled right out, and the outer end is shaped as in Fig. 26 to facilitate withdrawal.

Drawers.— These are dovetailed in the usual way. They work on runners screwed to top and bottom edges of side framing rails, the top runners being ¾ in. square, and those at the bottom 1 in. wide by ½ in. thick.

22

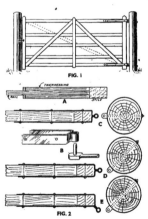

METHODS OF HANGING FIELD GATES.

FOLDING PICNIC TABLE

FOR picnics a light folding table which can be packed flat will be found a great convenience. For the size shown, 2 ft. 6 ins., these few parts are required :—

		ft.	ins.	ins.	ins.
4 Frame stiles	. .	2	6	3	$\frac{5}{8}$
4 Frame rails	. .	1	3	3	$\frac{5}{8}$
2 Tops (plywood)	. .	2	6	15	$\frac{3}{16}$
4 Legs	. . .	.	9	$1\frac{1}{8}$	$1\frac{1}{8}$
2 Leg rails	. .	2	3	$1\frac{1}{4}$	$\frac{1}{2}$
2 Spring laths	. .	1	3	3	$\frac{3}{8}$
2 Blocks for do.	. .		3	3	1
2 Slides (plywood)	. .	1	1	3	$\frac{3}{16}$
2 Battens	. .	2	3	1	1

Adjustable parts such as laths and slides should be measured from the job.

The Leaves (Fig. 2) are frames with half-lap corners covered with $\frac{3}{16}$ in. birch plywood. A wood light in weight is preferable. Glue and screw the corners, and secure the ply with fine panel pins after gluing down, punching home and stopping the holes. Hinge with back-flap hinges, bedded in. The slots for slides will be cut before the plywood is fixed.

THE TABLE SHOWN IS 2 FT. 6 INS. SQUARE, LEGS BEING 9 INS. HIGH. IT PACKS FLAT FOR CONVENIENT TRANSIT.

rail) keeps them flat. As the legs are raised the lath rises a little, slips over the edge, and then springs back to its normal position, thus preventing the legs from dropping down. By means of the laths and battens the legs are kept rigid in either position.

The laths are screwed to blocks 3 ins. square to raise them to the correct height. Thickness of these is about 1 in., but must be tested. Screw each lath with *four* screws.

Slides.—These are required so that the top, when opened flat, presents an unyielding surface. In Fig. 2 two slides are shown, these being of $\frac{3}{16}$ in. five-ply. Length is about 13 ins., but must be measured from the job. A width of 3 ins. will do; the essential matter is that they are rigid. The inner framing stiles are halved to receive them (see Fig. 4), whilst the outer stiles are notched about $\frac{3}{8}$ in. to take the ends when the table is folded. A 1 in. length of $\frac{3}{4}$ in. dowel serves as a knob for handling, at the same time acting as a stop when the slides are pushed in to lock the two leaves. Fig. 2 shows how, when the table is opened, the slides are pushed in to lock the leaves. To close the table, pull back the slides, lift the spring laths,

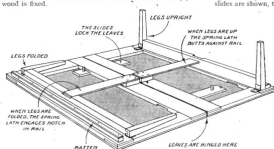

FIG. 1. THIS SHOWS UNDERSIDE OF TABLE WITH (*at left*) LEGS FOLDED, AND (*at right*) LEGS RAISED FOR USE.
The diagram also shows how the spring laths and the two centre slides operate.

Legs, finishing $1\frac{1}{8}$ ins. square, look better if tapered. Each pair is connected by a rail (Fig. 4) dovetailed as indicated. Legs stand in $1\frac{1}{2}$ ins. from side edges of legs, the length over each pair thus being 27 ins. Note the position of back-flap hinges (Fig. 2). To keep legs from splaying backwards a batten is screwed to the framework $\frac{1}{4}$ in. from the edge. This may be of 1 in. square stuff with outer top edges chamfered, the face next legs being kept square. When legs are up they should butt dead against this batten ; then if legs are $1\frac{1}{8}$ ins. square the distance between leg and batten (when folded) will be $1\frac{3}{8}$ ins.

Spring Laths.—The legs, when either up or down, are kept in position by means of two laths which act as springs. The exact length of these will be determined when fitting, but they are approximately $12\frac{1}{2}$ ins., and may be of oak $2\frac{1}{2}$ ins. or 3 ins. wide by $\frac{3}{16}$ in. thick. When legs are folded, the lath (engaging a notch in outer face of

press down the legs, and fold the leaves flat. As the slides engage slots at both ends they do not come loose. A hook and eye or a small leather strap may be fitted to hold all together.

To finish the table use either paint, lacquer, or a heat-resistant varnish. Separate the parts as far as possible first.

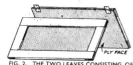

FIG. 2. THE TWO LEAVES CONSISTING OF FRAMES FACED WITH PLYWOOD.

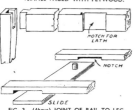

FIG. 3. (*Above*) JOINT OF RAIL TO LEG. (*Below*) HOW THE SLIDES WORK.

FENCING for GARDEN or ALLOTMENT

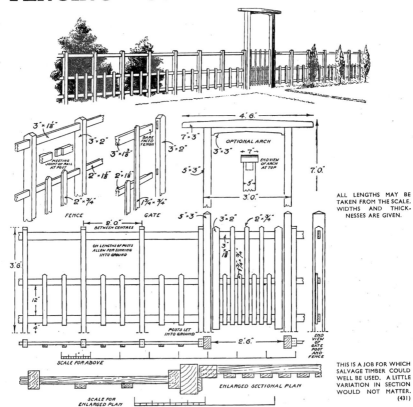

ALL LENGTHS MAY BE TAKEN FROM THE SCALE. WIDTHS AND THICKNESSES ARE GIVEN.

THIS IS A JOB FOR WHICH SALVAGE TIMBER COULD WELL BE USED. A LITTLE VARIATION IN SECTION WOULD NOT MATTER.
(431)

GARDEN TRELLIS
(See illustrations on opposite page)

Fig. 1.—Arch may be 7 ft. 6 ins. to 8 ft. high, with width of 3 ft. 6 ins. to 4 ft. Posts 2½ ins. square, sunk 18 ins. into ground. Width over ends 16 ins. to 18 ins. Post heads, 4 ins. by 2½ ins., projecting 6 ins. at each side. Rails, 2½ ins. by 2 ins. Laths, 1½ ins. by ⅝ in. Top bars 2½ ins. by 1½ ins. Use red deal.

Fig. 2.—Sizes of timbers : (A) 4 ins. square. (B) 4 ins. square. (C) 3 ins. by 4 ins. (D) 2 ins. square. (E) 2½ ins. square. (F) 2 ins. by 2½ ins. (G) 1¾ ins. by ⅝ in. Gate stiles and rails, 3 ins. by 2 ins. Mid rail, 2 ins. by 2 ins. Slats, 2 ins. by 1½ ins. Boarding, ⅝ in. (See scale for general dimensions.)

Fig. 3.—Posts, 3 ins. to 4 ins. square, according to height. Trellis rails, 2 ins. thick, chamfered. Trellis, ⅞ in. by ⅜ in. Height to top of trellis, 4 ft. 6 ins. to 6 ft.

Fig. 4.—Posts, 3 ins. square. Rails, 2½ ins. by 2½ ins. Laths, 1½ ins. by ¾ in. This spacing must be worked out carefully.

Fig. 5.—Posts and rails, 3 ins. square. Trellis, ⅞ in. by ½ in.

Fig. 6.—Posts and rails, 2½ ins. to 3 ins. square, according to height. Trellis, ⅞ in. by ⅜ in.

Fig. 7.—Posts and rails, 2½ ins. or 2¼ ins. Trellis, ¾ in. by ⅜ in. Circle may be bent (hoop fashion) from thin lath.

Note that the thicknesses of timber may be reduced for screens smaller than those shown.

24

GARDEN TRELLIS

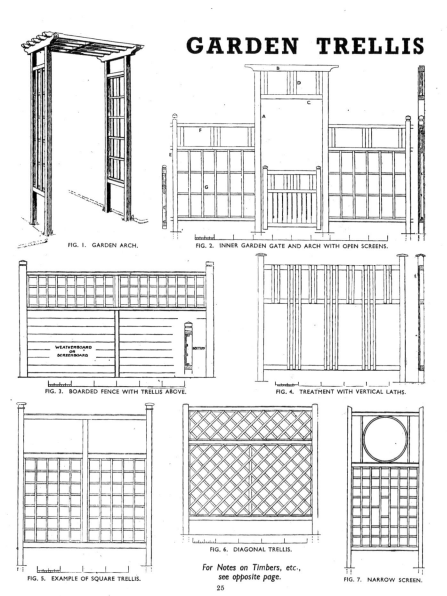

FIG. 1. GARDEN ARCH.

FIG. 2. INNER GARDEN GATE AND ARCH WITH OPEN SCREENS.

FIG. 3. BOARDED FENCE WITH TRELLIS ABOVE.

WEATHERBOARD OR SCREENBOARD

SECTION

FIG. 4. TREATMENT WITH VERTICAL LATHS.

FIG. 5. EXAMPLE OF SQUARE TRELLIS.

FIG. 6. DIAGONAL TRELLIS.

FIG. 7. NARROW SCREEN.

For Notes on Timbers, etc.,
see opposite page.

25

OBSERVATION BEEHIVE
ALTERNATIVELY HOW TO CONVERT AN EXISTING ONE

EVEN through an ideal observation beehive made entirely of clear glass it would be difficult to see the bee actually at work in its cell. Bees like warmth, darkness, and privacy in which to carry on their communal task and resent any interference with these conditions although quite adaptable in other ways. Still it is possible to see something of the bees' activities, especially in a strong colony, by putting clear glass windows into the front and rear of a National Hive. This is not entirely satisfactory from the observational point of view but is the best that can be done. In this design we show windows inserted at front and rear of an ordinary standard beehive (W. B. C. Pattern). The modern beehive consists of four or more separate sections, floorboard, brood chamber, lift or lifts, and roof. As the lift is similar to the brood chamber but for the entrance it is omitted in the working sketch, Fig. 2. Between the brood chamber where the queen lays her eggs and the lift (or super) is fitted a queen excluder which allows the working bees to pass but not the queen, owing to her size. This is a slotted zinc plate or galvanised grill.

Construction. —The walls of the roof, lift, and brood chamber should be through-dovetailed together, using paint or waterproof glue when assembling. The edges of each should meet perfectly with a good close joint but should be bevelled, Fig. 2, so that the plinth of an upper section does not bind upon expansion. The slopes needed for the roof boards should be sawn and planed after assembly. The roof should have ample overhang, say 3 ins. at front and rear and 2 ins. at sides, to carry off rainwater and is nailed or screwed on.

Floor Board (Fig. 2) is nailed or screwed to stout battens (A) which are notched and tapered for the alighting board. The boards forming the floor should finish as stout as possible from 1 inch stuff and the joints should be tongued.

Body Boxes (Fig. 2) that fit inside lift and brood chamber are similar excepting that the lower one will be cut away along the front bottom edge to form an entrance lineable with the outer case. The entrance is boxed in between the body box and outer case to prevent bees getting in the cavity between the inner and outer walls. The body box differs from the usual type by the substitution of rails (R), Fig. 2, for the usual solid front and ┌ back. These rails are tenoned through the side of the box and rebated for glass. Blocks screwed on each side of the glass into the sides of the box keep it in position. Arrange so that the glass can be removed at any time for cleaning or converting.

Keep the aperture as large as possible so that the frames are fully visible. The *inside* sizes shown on the sketch are important, for the standard British frame to take comb

(*Continued on page 27*).

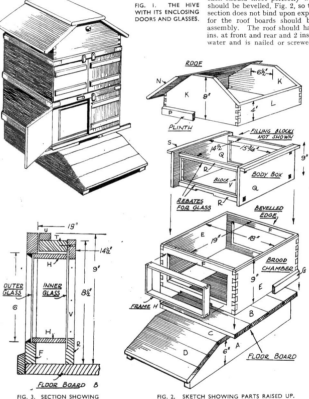

FIG. 1.   THE HIVE WITH ITS ENCLOSING DOORS AND GLASSES.

FIG. 3. SECTION SHOWING GLASS FRAMES.

FIG. 2.   SKETCH SHOWING PARTS RAISED UP.
Parts include floor board, brood chamber, lift, and roof.

DOUBLE FOLDING GARDEN STEPS

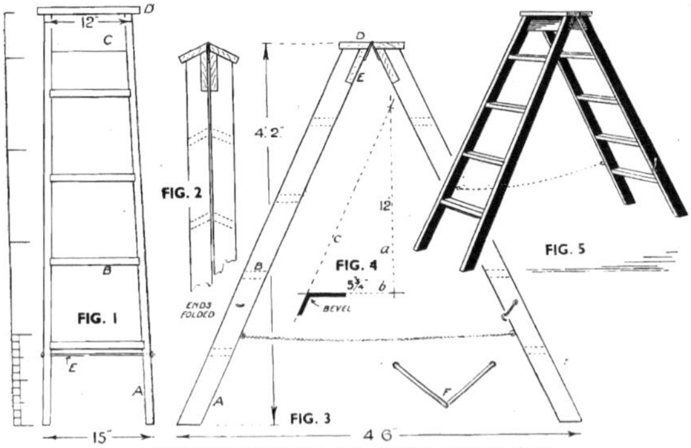

ELEVATIONS SHOWING THE GENERAL SETTING OUT.
Height of Steps when open, 4 ft. 2 ins.

FOLDING garden steps may not often be seen, but they are very handy for pruning tall hedges and for pulling fruit.

The smallest really useful size worth making would be steps of a height of from 4 ft. to 4 ft. 3 ins. when open.

Use ash, birch, or beech, regarding the thicknesses as net. In larch— a good substitute—thicknesses are better at 1 in. net. In setting out, the one preliminary point where care is essential is in securing the bevel for the steps. The angle for the ladder when open (given at Fig. 3) is a convenient one, and the bevel may be ascertained by following the diagram at Fig. 4. Draw lines *a* and *b* at right angles to each other, making *a* 12 ins. long and *b* 5¼ ins. Draw the connecting line *c*, and if this is projected at the foot you have the correct bevel shown by the heavy black line. The angle may be taken off on the joiner's bevel, or, failing this, a templet may be cut in thin plywood and used for marking the sides (A).

From Fig. 1 it will be noticed that (on front elevation) the steps taper from 15 ins. at ground to 12 ins. at top. The grooves for treads are cut 3/16 in. deep, but, on account of the taper, the treads enter slightly on the bevel. The actual bevel is almost negligible and may be guessed. Indeed, the common workshop practice is to fit in the bottom-tread and top board by trial and then (by the try-and-fit method) fix in the intermediate treads. Each tread is held by three nails at each side these being driven in slightly askew.

The back boards (C) are let in and screwed. The top boards (D), over-lapping 1 in. at sides and ½ in. at front, are trenched to take the sides and then nailed on. Underneath the bottom tread it is usual to fit a stiffening iron rod (E), say ⅜ in. in diameter, threaded for a nut. The two completed sides are hinged with a pair of stout iron back-flap hinges.

The double steps must have a stout cord attached as shown to prevent any chance of slipping when open. An alternative is an iron stay (F, Fig. 3) fitted to sides about 18 ins. from top. A hook and staple may be provided to hold them when folded.

Light material may be used throughout, the parts required being these :—

		ft.	ins.	ins.	ins.
(A)	4 Sides	4	8	3	⅞
(B)	8 Treads	1	1	4	⅞
(C)	2 Back boards . . .	1	1	5	⅞
(D)	2 Top boards . . .	1	2	4¼	⅞

OBSERVATION BEEHIVE

(Cont. from page 26)

foundations measures 14 ins. by 8½ ins. high by 17 ins. over-all length along the top. The box will accommodate ten comb frames spaced about ⅜ in. apart. Blocks (T and U) are added at front and back of the boxes to fill in the cavity and position the frames in the box.

Now with a pad saw cut openings in the front and rear of the brood chamber and lift. The openings should be as large as possible, say 15 ins. long by about 6 ins. high. Into these openings we slip a box frame about ⅜ ins. thick to sit up tight against the glass in the body box (Fig. 3). The front edges of the frames are set back to allow the outer glass to be bradded and puttied in. Shutters are necessary and these can be a sliding metal type or hinged wooden doors battened on the front and secured with turn-buttons as shown in the sketch, Fig. 1.

Different types of hives will require a somewhat different treatment and this is, more or less, a suggestion only.

CUTTING LIST

		Long ft.	Long ins.	Wide ins.	Thick ins.
Floor Board—					
A	2 Battens	3	0	6	1⅜
	2 Cross rails . . .	1	3	6	1⅛
B	1 Floor	1	7½	20½	¾
C	1 Alighting Bd. . . .	1	6	5	¾
D	1 Ditto	1	6	14	¾
Brood Chamber and Lift, for each—					
E	2 Sides	1	8½	9	¾
F	2 Front and back . . .	1	7½	9	¾
G	2 Plinths	1	9¾	2	⅝
	2 Ditto	1	8¾	2	⅝
H	4 For frames . . .	1	3	2	⅜
	4 Ditto		6	2	⅜
Roof—					
K	2 Front and back . . .	1	7½	9	¾
L	2 Sides	1	8½	4½	¾
M	1 Roof	2	2½	10½	¾
N	2 Roof	2	2½	10½	¾
P	2 Plinths	1	9¾	2	⅝
	2 Ditto	1	8¾	2	⅝
Body Boxes, for each—					
Q	2 Sides	1	7	9	½
R	4 Front and back rails . .	1	4¾	1¾	⅝
S	2 Side fillings . . .	1	7	¾	⅝
T	2 Blocks	1	3¾	1⅝	¾
U	2 Ditto	1	3¾	⅞	⅝
V	8 Glass fillets . . .		6	⅝	⅝

All sizes are net.

BIRD-NESTING HOUSE

THE house shown calls for little description. Base (A) may be a solid ⅜ in. board, or of ½ in. tongued and grooved boarding with two battens underneath. A size of 15 ins. by 11 ins. is suggested.

For ends (B) two pieces of ½ in. stuff about 7¼ ins. high by 8¼ ins. wide are required, and for front and back (C and D) two ⅜ in. pieces 13 ins. by 7¼ ins. Front and back overlap ends, to which they are nailed. If thought necessary lengths of 7¼ ins. angle moulding may be nailed in inside corners. In front (C) a doorway 6 ins. by 2½ ins. is pierced, leaving a step ½ in. high (see dotted line Fig. 1). The back is plain. Any windows shown are intended to be painted in.

The front (C) has an overlay panel (E) pinned to it. This may be of ½ in. wood, 7¼ ins. by 5 ins., cut with an arched doorway 5½ ins. by 3 ins.

(Fig. 5). All four sides of house will be bevelled to suit slope of roof.

Roof.—This is supported by two pieces (F and G, Fig. 5). These are 2¼ ins. wide from ½ in. stuff and will be cut to fit. In elevation they are seen in Figs. 2 and 3. The cross lengths (G) are halved to (F) and may be housed or nailed to house sides. Top edge (F) will be bevelled on both sides to agree with roof boards.

The roof itself will be fitted from the job, but it will be a help to set out the general plan (Fig. 4) on a sheet of stiff paper or thin card. Square this to 16½ ins. by 12½ ins., draw a centre line and set out the side lengths of 15 ins. and the end lengths of 11 ins. A trial fit will enable you to set out each piece. First fix down the two large side pieces and then trim the end pieces to a fit. House sides and roof supports give an ample bearing. Use ¼ in. ply and cover with light waterproof.

Chimney (H) is 2 ins. by 1¼ ins. by ⅞ in., screwed from below. Pot may be a ½ in. length of ¾ in. dowel rod.

Pole.—This may be of 2 ins. by 2 ins. or of 3 ins. square, tapering to 2 ins. Allow a height of, say, 6 ft. 6 ins. from ground to base of house, an extra 18 ins. being allowed for entering ground.

Two ⅞ in. bracket pieces, 8 ins. by 4 ins. (J, Fig. 5) may be cut for supporting the house. The brackets are halved to each other and the whole then cross-halved to top of pole. Four braces (K) may be fitted in the angles if wanted, and through them the house screwed in position.

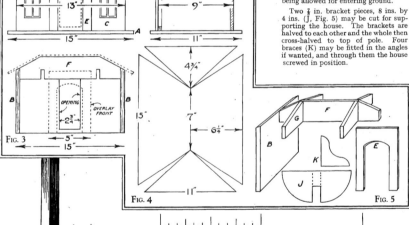

POLE BIRD HOUSE. Size of House (Carcase), 13 ins. by 9 ins. Length of Pole may be 6 ft. (or more) from ground. FIG. 1. FRONT ELEVATION. FIG. 2. SECTIONAL END VIEW. FIG. 3. SECTIONAL VIEW SHOWING ROOF SUPPORT. FIG. 4. PLAN OF ROOF PARTS. FIG. 5. ROOF SUPPORTS, POLE BRACKETS AND OVERLAY FRONT.

28

CHILDREN'S GARDEN

PLAY TABLE AND CHAIRS

F OR these light pieces any sound, straight-grained hardwood may be used, oak naturally being the first choice.

Table.—Squares 1⅜ ins. by 1⅜ ins. are used for the legs. Each leg is mortised on one face for front and back top rails (B, Fig. 6) ; also, on the other inside face, dovetail-slotted for the flat end rails (C) and mortised for tenons on under cross rails (E).

End rails (C) are kept 4 ins. wide so that they may be lap-dovetailed both to legs and to long top rails (B). A centre rail (D), also lap-dovetailed to top rails (B), stiffens the whole and provides an extra bearing for the slatted top. The stretcher (F) acts as a further stiffener.

FIG. I. CHILDREN'S GARDEN PLAY TABLE AND CHAIRS.
Size of Table, 28 ins. by 16 ins. by 24 ins. high.

CUTTING LIST

Table—		ft. ins.	ins.	ins.
(A)	4 Legs . .	2 0	1⅜	1⅜
(B)	2 Top rails .	2 2	2	⅞
(C)	2 End top rails	1 4	4	⅞
(D)	Centre top rail	1 3	2½	⅞
(E)	Under cross rail	1 4	1¼	⅞
(F)	Stretcher .	2 2	1¼	¾
(G)	8 Top slats .	2 4	1⅜	½

Chair (each)—		ft. ins.	ins.	ins.
(H)	2 Back legs	1 10	1⅜	1⅜

		ft. ins.	ins.	ins.
(I)	2 Front legs	1 2	1⅜	1⅜
(K)	2 Seat rails	1 0	1½	⅞
(L)	2 Ditto	1 1	1½	⅞
(M)	2 Under rails	1 1	1¼	¾
(N)	Stretcher .	1 0	1¼	¾
(O)	Back rail	1 3	2	⅞
(P)	7 Seat laths	1 0	1½	½

Lengths allow for joints and trimming but all thicknesses are net.

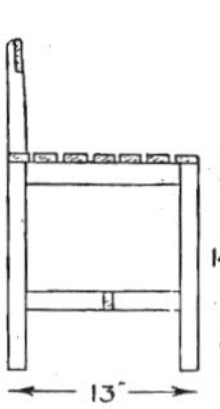

Top slats, or laths, are spaced equally and are screwed from below with flat-headed brass screws, well countersunk. Ease all upper edges with glasspaper.

Chairs.—These, with seats 12 ins. by 13 ins. and 14½ ins. from ground, are planned to fit between legs at end and clear the table cross rail (E).

The chair seat rails (K and L, Fig. 7) are securely tenoned to legs and braced in the angles. The back legs (H) do not require a rake, as depth (front to back) of seat is an inch more than the width. It is wise, however, to taper the back legs from seat line upwards as shown. The underframe rails (M) and stretcher (N) are tenoned. The top back rail (O) is halved to back legs so that it will fit flush. It may be pegged on, or screwed with brass screws from behind. The seat laths (P) will also be held with brass screws.

GLAZING HINT

Many practical men consider that when glazing a greenhouse roof it is a mistake to put a corner of putty at the *outside*. The reason is that it is liable to crack, and dampness settling in the openings may attack the wood and cause rot. It is generally enough to put a bed of putty in the rebate and press in the glass, trimming off neatly the squeezed-out surplus. It is essential that the rebate is painted before the putty is applied as otherwise the bare wood is liable to soak up the oil from the putty with the result that the latter does not stick.

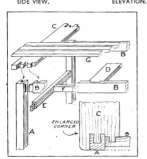

FIG 2. CHAIR : SIDE VIEW.

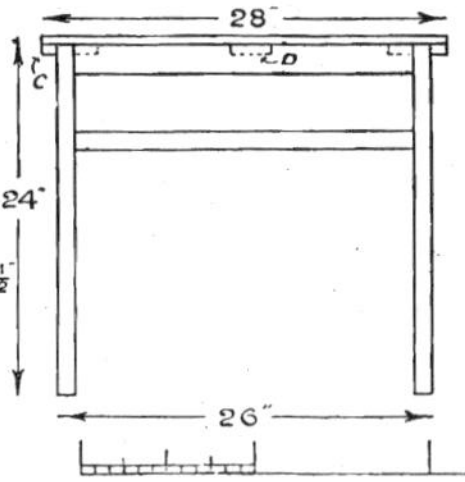

FIG. 3. TABLE : ELEVATION.

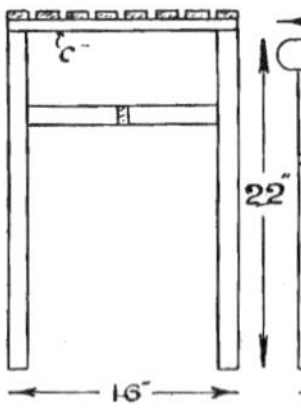

FIG. 4. TABLE : END VIEW.

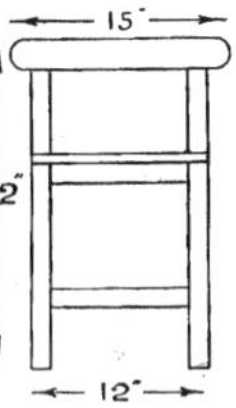

FIG. 5. CHAIR : FRONT VIEW.

FIG. 6. DETAIL OF TABLE.

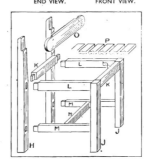

FIG. 7. DETAIL OF CHAIR.

The usual form of wheelbarrow with its wheel right at the front has the advantage of simplicity, but anyone who has had to wheel heavy loads knows that it can be very tiring owing to so much of the weight having to be taken by the arms of the user. In the design shown in Fig. I the wheel is set back from the front so that it takes a much larger share of the weight. A little adjustment of the wheel back or forth will show the best position.

IF you can obtain a reliable hardwood for the frame—ash or beech—use it. Otherwise deal, if reasonably free from knots, makes a quite sound job. Set it out in full size as at F, Fig. 2, so that exact sizes and angles can be obtained. The adjustable bevel should be set so that the joints can be marked. Failing this, a template of the angle can be cut in stout card or ply. The strongest joint is the mortise and tenon, taken right through and wedged. Otherwise the simple grooved joint as shown makes a simple alternative.

The handles are worked to a convenient and comfortable shape (see B), and are rounded over as shown.

Use paint when assembling and drive in good stout nails, allowing them to slope at alternate angles, thus exerting a dovetail grip. Test for squareness with a diagonal rod.

Wheel. — A reliable wheel is made by mitreing together four pieces (the felloes), strengthening the joints with loose tongues at C and D. They can be 3 ins. wide by 2 to 2½ ins. thick to make a wheel 12 ins. in diameter. Spokes are 2 ins. square, and are tenoned into the felloes. They are halved where they intersect. Assemble with paint and when dry mark out and cut the circular shape, finishing off with spokeshave or plane. Finally mark the centre by using the gauge from four or five positions around the wheel, and bore in from each side to take a ⅝ in. or ¾ in. iron axle.

At each side a wood block is fitted as at D, the thickness depending upon the distance between the two blocks fixed to the frame in which the axle is pivoted. Knock the axle (a good tight fit) into the wheel, bore holes in the blocks and pass them on from each side. Paint the joining surfaces and secure with skew nails. These blocks serve to keep the wheel in position laterally, and also to stiffen the wheel on its axle. A simple wheel made of three pieces laminated together is given at E. The parts are put together and the shape cut afterwards.

WHEELBARROW

Wheel Blocks.—These, shown at B and F, Fig. 2, are 3 ins. thick and are tapered towards the front so that their inner surfaces are parallel when in position (see F). The depth can be 8 ins., this allowing the wheel to clear the barrow bottom by about 1 in. It may be necessary to chamfer the back edge of the front frame rail to give clearance here. Remember that the holes for the axle have to be bored square from the inner tapered surfaces. The size should allow a piece of brass tubing in which the axle fits to be inserted. It is knocked over at the ends to keep it in position.

Place the wheel with its axle in the blocks, and fix the last named in position with cramps. Test to see whether it gives comfortable balance, and when square drive in screws from the outside.

Legs.—These are double-notched to the frame as at B. The notches necessarily slope at an angle because the legs must be upright when the barrow is at rest. The handles might be about 18 ins. from the ground, and it will be found that an over-all height of 2 ft. 2 ins. is about right for the legs. Put the barrow on level ground with the arms raised to rest on an 18 in. high box, place the legs in position, upright, and mark where the parts intersect. Cut the notches and taper the upper ends so that the sides will lie comfortably against them. Bolts are used for fixing, washers being passed beneath the nuts so that they do not bite into the wood.

Upper Part.—Fit one side first. Bevel the lower side so that it fits snug on the framework, and cut off the ends at a slope. The exact slope is not important. It will probably be necessary to joint together two pieces to obtain the width. At the ends 1¼ in. square battens are nailed, the nails being taken right through and clenched. From this mark the other side, and fix both with nails to the tops of the legs. Skew nails can be used at the bottom for fixing to the framework.

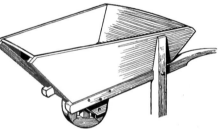

FIG. I. BARROW WITH WHEEL SET BACK FROM THE FRONT.
By fixing the wheel farther back a far greater proportion of the weight is taken from the arms, making the barrow far less tiring in use. The exact position is found by experiment. (See Fig. 2 on opposite page.)

The back and front can largely be fitted by trial and error, though it is a help to cut a template in cardboard. Once the angle and bevel have been obtained it will be a help in fitting a second piece. The angles of the front, of course, are different from those of the back. Drive nails through the sides into front and back, and also insert nails into the battens. The bottom consists of plain boards fitted to rest directly on the framework, the grain running from side to side.

If you have used deal for the barrow give it a yearly coat of creosote, paying special attention to the end grain. It will help to preserve the wood. One other point. As deal does not hold nails specially well, drive them in in alternate directions so that they have a dovetail grip.

WOOD PRESERVATIVES

FOR a preservative to be thoroughly effective it must penetrate right through the timber, and to do this some form of vacuum impregnating plant is essential. The only practical way, however, for the average man is to coat the surface with a brush, which coat has only a very limited penetration and therefore a limited preservative action.

The best known and one of the most effective is creosote, which is a distillate of coal tar and is a brownish black oil. This is best applied with a brush and serves the double purpose of staining and preserving. Its water-proofing qualities are negligible, it only preventing the attack of fungoid growths due to dampness. If thinned with petroleum the mixture tends to make splitting less likely owing to increased moisture-proofing qualities, and increases penetration. This oil dries very slowly and on this account tends to creep, so that care should be taken that it is not close to any plaster or there is a danger of staining. Owing to its strong smell it should not be used for preserving the timbers of food-safes and the like. When thoroughly dry it can, however, be painted over with outdoor paint, which will weather the timber properly if not allowed to scale off.

For thorough impregnation the Forest Products Research Laboratory recommend the following method for posts to be buried in the earth. The timber is immersed in a tank of creosote and heated up to 180-200 degrees F. After being maintained at this heat for about an hour it is allowed to cool and the timber then removed. It is in the cooling period that the absorption takes place.

Other preservatives are water soluble, which are objectionable on account of their being washed out easily by rain, but are nearly all capable of being painted which prevents this washing out. Zinc chloride in a five per cent. solution is an ideal preservative, but has a corrosive action on metal. This can be largely prevented by well coating bolts and similar fittings with white lead. Due to this corrosion the solution must not be used stronger. Copper sulphate in about the same strength can also be used, as it is highly poisonous to fungoid growth, but has also a corrosive action.

The type known as solvent preservatives are those where a poisonous chemical is dissolved in some volatile oil or spirit. On application to the timber the solvent evaporates, leaving the chemical in the pores. Due to the use of naphtha and similar oils, these preservatives penetrate rather more deeply than do the water soluble types, but owing to the relatively high prices of many of the organic salts and solvents their application is rather limited.

Many of the proprietary brands on the market are of this type and very reliable, as also are several of those of an oily nature. A large number are coloured with some pigment, making the timber so coated more attractive.

Regarding the staining and finishing of outdoor woodwork, water stains, obtainable in almost any colour, are the best for every purpose. Oil stains are made chiefly from aniline or coal tar dyes and are mostly very fugitive when directly in contact with strong sunlight. The water stains are of real value on finished timber only, creosote being much the best stain for all rough work apart from flower boxes, greenhouse timbers and so on, where this oil is injurious to plant life. If these stains are well cut down after drying they may be coated with a good outdoor oil varnish, which will increase the weathering and bring out any attractive features of the grain.

In the case of timber of great natural durability, such as oak, staining and subsequent rubbing in of linseed oil several times is quite good.

Paint properly applied is a good method of preventing the action of the weather and the ground coat should be half red lead and half white lead, used very thinly with turps at first to ensure penetration of the wood. Use one or more subsequent coats of white lead, finishing with some suitable outdoor lead paint of required colour.

With regard to posts sunk into the ground, the timber may be either well coated with creosote as previously described, or burned partly on the surface (to kill any destroying fungus) and well coated afterwards with pitch.

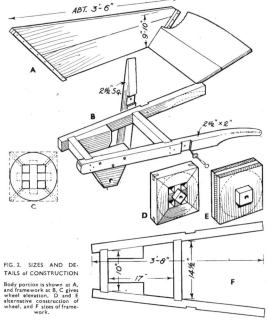

ABT. 3'-6"

9'-10"

2½" Sq.

2½" × 2"

A

B

C

D

E

3'-8"

17"

14½"

F

FIG. 2. SIZES AND DETAILS of CONSTRUCTION

Body portion is shown at A, and framework at B, C gives wheel elevation, D and E alternative construction of wheel, and F sizes of framework.

SUBSTITUTES FOR WOOD

GALVANISED IRON AND ASBESTOS-CEMENT SHEET

THE timber shortage has made the erection of small buildings such as Coal Houses, Cycle Sheds, Summer Houses, Garages, and Workshops difficult. Many have sought a substitute for wood in galvanised iron corrugated sheets which answer quite well for such buildings as Coal Houses and Cycle Sheds.

Corrugated Iron.—Corrugated iron sheets are obtainable in widths of 2 ft. ranging up to about 3 ft. 6 ins., but the narrower width is most common, while lengths range from 4 ft. to 12 ft. The sheets must be properly supported with wood framings when the sides of a building are being covered, and with purlins in the case of a roof, placed at intervals of about 3 ft., as shown in Fig. 1. In

both cases it is better to screw the sheets to the wood rather than nail them, the screws being driven through the crown or apex of the corrugations (not in the channels). Washers are placed under the screw-heads. Both screws and washers should be galvanised to prevent rusting. The holes should be carefully marked where required, and the sheet laid with the convex side on a block of wood for punching with a steel punch. Wherever possible it is better to use a single long sheet instead of two short ones to avoid a joint, but where two sheets are necessary to make the length the lap should not be less than 6 ins. In cases where small sheets are required it may be necessary to cut, but as this is a rather troublesome operation it may be possible to overcome the difficulty by allowing a

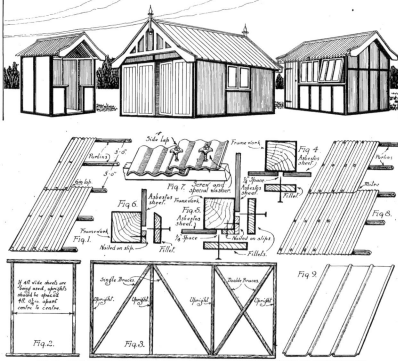

SUMMER HOUSE, GARAGE, AND GARDEN SHED, ALL FITTED WITH CORRUGATED IRON OR ASBESTOS ROOFS.
Note that the asbestos-cement sheet can be obtained in flat sheets and in two different patterns of corrugations (see Figs. 8 and 9).

THESE MATERIALS MAKE EXCELLENT ROOFINGS AND PANELS

longer lap. The lap for sheets placed side to side should be one and a half corrugations, screws being driven through both sheets.

Asbestos-Cement Sheets.—While galvanised iron is quite suitable for the purposes previously mentioned, it is rather unsuitable for buildings such as Garages, Summer Houses, and Work-shops. As a substitute for wood the comparatively new product—asbestos-cement sheets—is very useful. There is a superficial resemblance between corrugated asbestos-cement sheets and corrugated iron, but the former has the advantage of being light, cheap, non-corrosive, heat, cold and fire resisting, while a building covered with corrugated iron is hot in summer and cold and damp with interior condensation in winter.

Plain asbestos-cement sheets are the most suitable for covering the sides of buildings, while corrugated sheets should be used for roofing. Different makes vary a little in dimensions, and before starting the framing of a building which is to be covered with the sheets it is advisable to obtain the exact sizes available. For covering the sides and ends of small buildings, sheets $\frac{1}{4}$ in. thick are suitable, and it is usually possible to obtain them in lengths of 4 ft., rising by successive 6 ins. up to 10 ft. long. It will be obvious that, providing the uprights in the framing are properly arranged, it will be possible to obtain sheets for covering any surface. Supposing 4 ft. wide sheets are being used, the uprights should be arranged at intervals of at least 4 ft. $\frac{1}{4}$ in. measuring from centre to centre, as shown in Fig. 2, to give a clearance of $\frac{1}{4}$ in. between the sheets. The over-all sizes as well, should, if feasible, be arranged to take two, three, or four sheets, as the case may be, without cutting, and the sizes of windows and doors should as far as possible be arranged with the same object in view.

Consideration of Strength.—Unlike wood boarding, which when nailed to the framework of a wood-framed building, greatly adds to its strength and rigidity, asbestos sheets need a strong, rigid framework to make them successful. For this purpose cross-bracing, or double cross-bracing, as shown in Fig. 3, should be introduced between the main framework wherever possible as this not only braces the building, but also strengthens the sheets. Another point to bear in mind is that asbestos sheets should not be rigidly fixed, or there will be a danger of the sheets cracking, because, while the asbestos sheets are not affected by heat or cold, the wood framework of the building contracts or expands with the changes in temperature. Hence it is a good plan to use as few nails as possible in the sheets themselves, but to fix them with wood fillets nailed outside, as shown in Fig. 4. If nails are used in the sheets it is advisable to drill holes slightly larger than the nails. By the use of fillets it is possible to fix the sheets without actually driving any nails through them. The fillets should be about 2 ins. wide by $\frac{1}{4}$ in. thick, the nails fixing the upright fillets being driven between the edges of the two meeting sheets. To make a sound job of the corners, and the top and bottom, it is a good plan to nail on thin slips of wood the same thickness as the sheets before fixing the fillets, as shown in Figs. 5 and 6, and it should be noted that the top edges of the bottom fillets should be slightly bevelled.

Corrugated Sheets.—Corrugated sheets are much stronger than flat sheets, so they should always be used for roofs. The corrugated sheets are also made in a number of convenient sizes, and if properly fixed offer complete resistance to the weather. Here again an effort should be made to use sheets as long as possible to obviate joints. The pitch of a roof in a moderately exposed pos-

ition should not be less than 30 degrees, and there should be a purlin every 3 ft. To fix the sheets to the purlins 3$\frac{1}{2}$ ins. galvanised screws with special washers as shown in Fig. 7 are used. Screw holes must be drilled through the crowns of the corrugations with a brace and bit, after the sheets have been temporarily fitted in place for marking these fixing holes. The sheets may be laid either from the right or left-hand side according to the prevailing direction of the wind. It is necessary to lap the sheets about one and a half corrugations—as with sheet iron, and the wind should not blow into the lap. Again, these corrugated sheets should not be too rigidly fixed otherwise there is a risk that they may be strained and may probably crack. The screw holes also should allow the screws to fit easily.

Sometimes in dealing with a wide lean-to roof it may be necessary to use two sheets to make its width. In this case two end sheets should be laid, the lower one first, then the one above allowing a 6 in. gap, but because of the two laps—lengthways and sideways—it is necessary to mitre the corners of the sheets. The first lower sheet is fixed without any cutting, but the sheet above must have the corner mitred 6 ins. long and about 4 ins. wide, and the next lower sheet is cut to correspond, this method of fitting and fixing being shown in Fig. 8. Another type of sheet measuring about 4 ft. long, has wide spaced corrugations, as shown in Fig. 9, and is of very pleasing appearance when fixed on a roof. In dealing with a ridge roof, ridge-pieces are available for every type of sheet.

The pleasing appearance of wood-framed buildings covered with asbestos sheets of various sizes is conveyed by the sketches showing one or two in their finished state. Some asbestos-cement products may be painted, others are best finished with cement wash. The wood strips used to fix the sheets should be painted a dark colour for effect.

Cutting Asbestos-Cement Sheets.—Avoid cutting where possible by arranging the work to suit the standard sizes. For small cuts a hack saw is excellent, but it is, of course, impossible to make a long cut with the tool. Any small-toothed saw answers the purpose, but avoid using best tools for the work. The substance is harder than wood and must be handled carefully to avoid cracks. Make sure it is well supported on a flat surface, and take special care when nearing the end of the cut. A narrow width may be cut by scribing well and breaking over a straight edge.

SHED DOORS

Where a shed door is constantly in use and is liable to swing open, it is best to provide some form of speedy attachment to keep it closed without the necessity of locking it. A button cut from 1 in. hardwood, is easily made and screwed to the post. Alternatively a metal one can be knocked up quickly from a strip of galvanised iron 1 in. wide of sufficient length—say 12 ins. to be doubled over on itself five or six times and be pressed flat in the vice or hammered. The button is then placed upon a block of wood and a hole punched, in it for screwing. Hook and eye attachment is also speedy in use and obtainable in various patterns and lengths. Where a door is padlocked a hasp and staple can be used as a neat fixing. Another method is to use two large galvanised eyes, one entered into the post and one into the door framing so that a chain can be passed through the eyes and secured by a padlock.

DESIGNS FOR LIGHT GARDEN GATES

THE eight designs shown are offered as suggestions, some suitable for light entrance gates, others for small inner gates dividing a vegetable from a flower garden. In height and width no two gates are exactly alike, but in each case it will be seen that, in spacing, it is easy to adapt the general design to a slightly different size, larger or smaller.

Entrance gates, which have to stand daily wear and tear

question of thickness may be left to the worker's judgment.

In every case the hanging (or hinged) stile is at the right. Whenever possible it is assumed that strap hinges are to be used.

General Hints on Construction.—If the gate is to be painted red, deal or larch may be used, all joints being held with thick paint instead of glue. In the case of a hard-

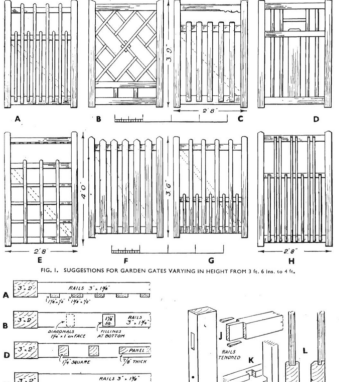

FIG. 1. SUGGESTIONS FOR GARDEN GATES VARYING IN HEIGHT FROM 3 ft. 6 ins. to 4 ft.

FIG. 2. PLANS OF THE VARIOUS GATES.

FIG. 3. THE CHIEF JOINTS USED.

(and sometimes rough usage), are usually stouter than secondary dividing gates, and where thicknesses are given the sizes apply to the former. For the lighter type the

wood, clear varnish is a customary finish, the joints being assembled with thick varnish. The tenons on rails will go right through the stiles and be wedged (see J, Fig. 3).

(Continued on page 35)

LIGHT TRANSPORT CART

FOR the body of this light cart ½ in. stuff should be adequate if sound. The sides are made to the shape and size shown in Fig. 2. Two pieces of wood could be used to make up the 18 in. width. Grooves ½ in. wide and ¼ in. deep are cut across each end ⅛ in. in from the edges, and battens 1¼ ins. wide are screwed on level with the inner edges of the grooves.

The front and back, which may also be in two widths, fit into the grooves in sides and are nailed to the battens.

Fig. 1.

FOR THE GARDEN, OR FOR SHOPPING.

Although not intended to take the place of the regular wheelbarrow, this cart has many garden uses and is inexpensive.

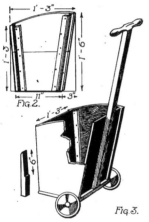

Fig. 2.

Fig. 3.

MAIN SIZES AND CONSTRUCTION.

The bottom is nailed to edges of sides, front and back, its edges (which are allowed to overhang slightly) being rounded. Hardwood is best for the single shaft; it is 2 ft. 9 ins. long by 1¼ ins. square. A cross handle about 8 ins. long with its ends conveniently shaped should be tenoned to top end, the completed shaft being bolted to the body.

A pair of disc wheels with a suitable axle are fixed under bottom as near the front as possible, and a leg is fitted at back so that the cart rests with its bottom in a horizontal position. The top end of the leg should be recessed and shaped as shown in Fig. 3 to allow for the back bevel of the body.

Painting, or varnishing, is necessary both for preservation and appearance.

LIGHT GARDEN GATES. *(Continued from page 34)*

Instead of wedging they are frequently pinned with hardwood pegs, the draw-bore method being adopted. When fitting the rails the stiles are left full in length top and bottom and trimmed later. This prevents the risk of a split.

For gates of the size indicated, stiles of 3 ins. by 2 ins. may be taken as adequately strong. The thickness of rails must necessarily vary. In the case of designs like A, F, G, and H, where slats are to be nailed on, the thickness of rails will be 1⅜ ins. or 1½ ins. Where, however, like B and D, the filling is tenoned in, a thickness of 1¾ ins. can be allowed. Again, in cases like C and E, the top rail may be 1¾ ins. or 2 ins. thick, while the mid and bottom rails are kept down to 1⅜ ins. or 1½ ins. For top and bottom rails a width of 3 ins. is ample, although in some cases the bottom rail (see A, C and H) is kept wider—say 3½ ins. or 4 ins. The sectional part plans in Fig. 2 will give a certain guidance as to the relation of rails to stiles.

Crossing parts such as the diagonal scheming in B will be halved at the intersections (K, Fig. 3). A panel as in D may be either housed in or fitted flush (L, Fig. 3). The upright fillings, square in section, of a gate like D, will be let in ½ in. top and bottom. It is customary very gently to chamfer off the top edges of rails to shed water.

Garden gates always stand up better to wear and tear if provided with a stiffening diagonal brace. See dotted lines on several of the diagrams. These, to ease the strain on the post, spring from the bottom of the hanging stile and are notched in at both ends.

If posts are partly supported by a brick or stone wall, squares of from 4 ins. to 5 ins. may be ample if the gate does not exceed about 3 ft. 9 ins. in height. Without such support they must be stouter, and in every case a length of at least 18 ins. should be allowed for entering the ground. Chamfered corners help to take off any appearance of heaviness. Posts should have cappings or be treated in some other way to prevent deterioration from water.

RUSTIC GARDEN FENCING

ASSUMING that straight larch and young pole will be used for a rustic fence of this type decide first on the thicknesses: This can be only approximate, the wood being in the rough and each length having a slight taper. For this reason take the mean thickness, remembering that the methods of fixing cannot be so strong and durable as in the case of squared timber.

Standards (A) may have a mean diameter of 3 ins. If to be 4 ft. long allow an extra 18 ins. for sinking in ground. Top and bottom rails (B) and intermediate uprights (C) may have a diameter of $2\frac{1}{2}$ ins., the remaining fillings (D) etc., being 2 ins. If there are to be gate posts (E) these must be stronger—say 5 ins. or 6 ins. One thing to remember when round timber is used is that the thickness appears the same from every point of view. In squared wood the thickness is increased when viewed from an angle.

Joints.—In rustic work we cannot have the durable dovetailed or tenoned fixtures that are possible with wrought timber. At the same time it may just be mentioned that, if rustic woodwork has fallen into disfavour, the reason probably is due to slipshod methods of fixing.

Three general points may be stressed. Firstly, remembering that rustic work is subject to the same strain that weather imposes on all other outdoor woodwork, decide on the most durable joint for the purpose and cut it as carefully as possible. As marking cannot be so accurate as on squared wood we must learn to be guided by the eye. Secondly, before assembling, thoroughly paint and creosote every part of a joint. If this is neglected rain will soon soak into any exposed nicks and provoke decay at the critical parts. Thirdly, use cut or wrought nails

as these hold better than round nails. Also, to avoid the risk of splitting, bore for every nail, and (if not too much trouble) have a small tin of tallow at hand so that the points may be dipped into this.

Assembling.—Taking the parts in order, the main uprights (A) will be sunk a full 18 ins. into the ground, the lower parts being tarred or creosoted. Round the tops. Various joints are shown in Fig. 2. The rails (B) are usually tenoned to the uprights as at (W), each meeting tenon being cut triangular in shape so that both will meet in the through mortise. Painting here is imperative, and each tenon may be held with a nail. Curved shoulders should be neatly trimmed so that the parts are a close fit.

The shorter uprights (C) may be either dowelled to the rails as at (V), or notched and nailed as at (Z). A tenoned joint (as at X) is sometimes used as an alternative. The tenon is often of the square stub form.

Where diagonals (D) cross, a halved joint is used as at U, the parts again being nailed. Where such diagonals meet the vertical or horizontal lengths they are notched in as at (Y). This is another joint which must be carefully cut if to last, any shrinkage being apt to wrench it loose.

For guidance, three alternative suggestions for panel fillings are given in Fig. 3.

Gate.—It may be added that a rustic fence does not necessarily mean that, if a gate is required, it also must be rustic. Indeed, the ordinary type looks better and is more useful. A gate 2 ft. 6 ins. wide may have stiles of 3 ins. by $1\frac{1}{2}$ ins. and rails 3 ins. by $1\frac{1}{2}$ ins. The brace may be $2\frac{1}{2}$ ins. by $\frac{7}{8}$ in. and the spars 2 ins. by $\frac{5}{8}$ in. Rails will enter the stiles with a bareface through tenon.

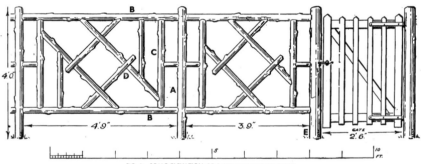

FIG. I. SCALE ELEVATION OF RUSTIC GARDEN FENCING.

FIG. 2. SOME RUSTIC WOODWORK JOINTS.

FIG. 3 ALTERNATIVE TREATMENT FOR PANELS
These panels are of the same proportion as the 3 ft. 9 ins. panel in Fig. I.

PIGEON COTE

BEFORE preparing or even deciding on the height of the pole for an outdoor erection of this kind it is wise to complete the actual cote. Quite obviously the size of this must be taken into consideration when determining the height from ground. The sizes suggested should be adapted to accommodate the number of birds the reader wishes to house.

Cote.—The actual size of this and the interior arrangement must be left to the worker to decide on the spot. As shown here it is a house (F) 18 ins. by 18 ins. and 13 ins. high, mounted on a boarded platform (D) 27 ins. by 27 ins. Above is a ceiling (G) 22 ins. by 22 ins. with pyramidal roof. From platform to top of finial (H) the height is about 2 ft.

The platform (D) is of ¾ in. boards, any width as convenient, tongued together and secured with two battens (E) of stuff 2 ins. by ⅞ in. The house sides (F) may also be of ¾ in. boards, each held by two 1¼ ins. by ¾ in. battens as shown. The four sides will be nailed together. Entrance openings are usually about 6 ins. by 4 ins. The boarded ceiling (G) may be of ⅝ in. boards nailed to the house. This ceiling overhangs the house about 2 ins. all round.

Roof.—A finial (H) 10 ins. or so long is squared to 1¼ ins. by 1¼ ins. and screwed to ceiling. The triangular pieces (J), 5 ins. high, are cut so that they will lie from corner to corner and are nailed on. In lengths they will be about 15

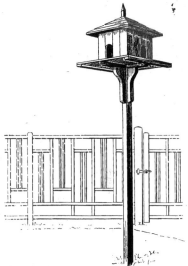

FIG. I. THE POLE COTE ERECTED IN THE GARDEN.
This gives a good idea of how attractive a feature the cote is. Suggested size of platform is 27 ins. square. Pole height should not be less than 6 ft.

ins. The roof weather-boarding may be of ⅛ in. and of whatever width is preferred. It is cut to fit and neatly bevelled at the corners. Allow a good overhang on all four sides so that the rain will not drip direct on the platform (D). The platform is sometimes bevelled away as at *a*, Fig. 2. A roofing felt is almost invariably added to prevent water from seeping into the house. The house is screwed to the platform from below.

Pole (A).—Generally speaking, 4 ins. by 4 ins. will do for this. A taper to 3 ins. by 3 ins. at top is well worth the extra trouble. Height from ground to platform (D) should never be less than 6 ft. and is sometimes as much as 8 ft. An average 6 ft. 6 ins. to 7 ft., but much depends on the surroundings. It is desirable that the cote should be within easy access. On the other hand, birds do not like cats to be prowling around too near. In length at least 2 ft. extra should be allowed for entering the ground. The sunk part is often strutted as at X, but a simpler plan is to nail on four 1 in. boards as at Z, each board being about 24 ins. by 6 ins. All sunk parts should be charred or tarred.

Supports (B) at top of pole may be 3 ins. or 3½ ins. wide by 2 ins. thick, halved where they intersect. Allow a length of 20 ins. at least and fix to a pole with a stout peg painted in. Brackets (C) may be 16 ins. by 5 ins., cut from 1½ ins. stuff. These may be tenoned or pegged to pole and supports or may simply be nailed. The platform is screwed to the supports from above.

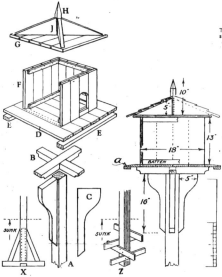

FIG. 2. HOW COTE AND POLE
ARE ASSEMBLED

FIG. 3. SCALE ELEVATION
WITH CHIEF SIZES

37

LIGHT CARPENTRY IN SPRING

TREADING BOARDS: BESOM BROOM: MULTIPLE DIBBLER: GARDEN BARROW

ALL this is quite simple work, but none the less useful. The items shown, moreover, can be made from scrap materials at hand.

Treading Boards (Fig. 1).—These may be made singly or in pairs to fit on the feet, and are most useful for levelling and firming ground where seeds have to be sown, or plants grown which need firm soil. The boards should be about 1 ft. 6 ins. long by 1 ft. wide and at least 1 in. thick, strengthened by nailing battens at the front and back. A width of 2 ins. will be sufficient for the front batten, but the back one should be 3 ins. wide because a recess has to be cut in it for the heel of the boot.

A leather strap is arranged for the toe, large enough to allow the boot to fit on some way. A most important point is to arrange the strap further back than the middle of the board so that the greatest weight is at the front, otherwise the board will drop every time the foot is raised.

Besom Broom (Fig. 2).—A good broom of this kind for sweeping paths and lawn may be made practically without cost as both the twigs for the broom head and a stick for the handle may be gathered in the country. Twigs of broom and birch are the most suitable because of their toughness, and they should be cut in lengths from 1 ft. 6 ins. to 2 ft. Sufficient are required to form a firm bundle from 5 ins. to 6 ins. in diameter at the head.

The most satisfactory method is to gather the twigs around a small stick, roughly tying them at first, and then finally securing with strands of wire, the ends of which should be twisted. The small stick is then withdrawn and the handle, about 3 ft. long by at least 1 in. diameter with the end pointed, is driven in to make a firm head and job.

Multiple Dibblers (Fig. 3).—Quite a simple dibbler may be made with a piece of wood about 1 ft. 6 ins. long by 3 ins. wide by 1 in. thick. A hand hole should be cut in the middle of the flat side, and the tool is completed by boring a number of pieces of ½ in. round rod into the edges.

On one side the rods could be spaced, say 3 ins. apart, and on the other side 4 ins., to make the dibbler adaptable. Another kind of dibbler may be made by boring a number of rods, say three rows, into a flat piece of board about 1 ft. 6 ins. long by 1 ft. wide, which should be strengthened with cross battens, and fitted with a suitable handle.

Light Barrow (Fig. 4).—A barrow of this light type is always convenient in the small garden. It may be made from any kind of 1 in. stuff. The two sides are shaped as shown, and battens 2 ins. wide are nailed at the bottom and back 1 in. from the edges. The sides are made as a pair.

The barrow should be mounted on a pair of low rubber-tyred wheels (about 6 ins. to 8 ins. diameter) and axle. Procure these before starting on the woodwork. An axle 1 ft. 6 ins. long between the collars would be ideal because the body could be 1 ft. 6 ins. wide. The bottom and back are nailed between the sides, and a top board 6 ins. wide is nailed above.

(Continued on page 39).

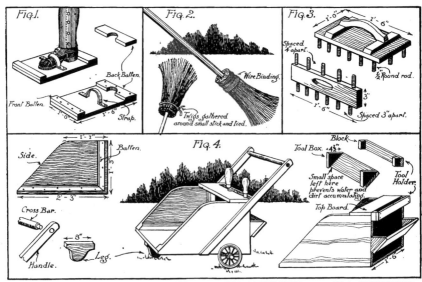

FIG. 1. TREADING BOARDS.   FIG. 2. BESOM BROOM.   FIG. 3. MULTIPLE DIBBLER.   FIG. 4. GARDEN BARROW.

LIGHT-WEIGHT
GARDEN LADDER

For those who need a garden ladder of light type the details given here will be of interest. Length may be anything from 5 ft. to 8 ft., but a useful average is 6 ft. 6 ins. or 7 ft. The construction may be explained in a word. Each side is built up with two lengths (A) of $\frac{7}{8}$ in. square stuff, bent and bolted at the ends, these being connected by cross-blocks (B) which are tenoned in. To these cross blocks the rungs (D) are tenoned and wedged. The result is a light, serviceable and strong ladder.

Sides.—Here the rim lengths (A) will be of ash, which is tough, durable and easily bent without steaming. The stuff must be straight grained and well seasoned, and may finish $\frac{7}{8}$ in. by $\frac{7}{8}$ in., or $1\frac{1}{4}$ ins. wide by $\frac{7}{8}$ in. thick. Necessarily, in planning, the lengths must be true.

The cross-blocks which bind the rims are of $\frac{7}{8}$ in. hardwood, and are tenoned right through and wedged as shown at B (Fig. 3). In width they may be 4 ins. First prepare the middle block and temporarily tenon it to the rims (A). Then cut the two wedge-shaped end blocks (C) about 6 ins. long, these tapering from about $1\frac{1}{4}$ ins. to $\frac{1}{4}$ in. at the point. Bore for two bolts at each end, and temporarily fit the bolts so that the complete side is bent to the required shape. The bolts may be either threaded for nuts, or of the type which are riveted over washers.

Obviously the intermediate cross-blocks (B) vary in height, whilst on account of the curve the shoulder angle is slightly different in each case. If, however, the centre block is cut square and the rims (A) bent up to the end triangular pieces, the other blocks could be placed in position and the shoulder angles marked individually.

Later, the bolts are withdrawn, the seven blocks (B) fitted, and the triangular end pieces (C) glued in and bolted. The intermediate blocks would then be wedged tightly and the rims cleaned up.

Rungs (or treads, D) may be round or square. If round they may be straight in length or curved (see Fig. 3). Stuff $1\frac{1}{4}$ ins. by $1\frac{1}{4}$ ins. is suitable for a ladder of 7 ft., but $1\frac{1}{4}$ ins. by $1\frac{1}{4}$ ins. would serve if oak, ash, or beech is used. The rungs are tenoned right through and wedged.

FIG. I. USEFUL GARDEN LADDER.
The suggested length of 7 ft. can be adapted within a little if required.

The finished ladder looks well, and if required for household use it may be painted or varnished.

LIGHT CARPENTRY
(Continued from page 38).

A tool holder may be formed behind this top board by nailing a strip of wood across the back and inserting two small blocks of wood between it and the back of the barrow, as shown in the details. A triangular, or even square tool box could be provided below if two triangular pieces, covered with a flat board, are nailed on. The wheels and axle should be kept well towards the back, and a small leg is fitted under the front to keep the barrow level when standing.

The handles should be $1\frac{1}{2}$ ins. wide by 1 in. thick, and long enough to stand about 2 ft. 6 ins. from the ground measuring perpendicularly. A cross bar $1\frac{1}{4}$ ins. diameter, is fitted between the ends of the handles. It should be shouldered, bored in, and nailed.

FIG. 3.
WEDGED
BLOCKS
AND
RUNGS.

D

B

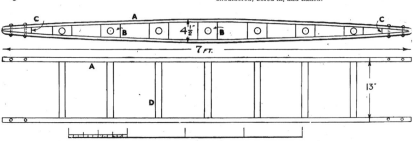

FIG. 2. ELEVATION AND SIDE VIEW. B AND C ARE CROSS-BLOCKS WHICH BIND THE RIMS A.

ENTRANCE GATE

SUITABLE FOR SUBURBAN BUNGALOW OR COTTAGE

FIG. I. GARDEN GATE OF CHARACTER.
Sizes shown are 3 ft. wide by 5 ft. 6 ins. high. The side trellis is optional.
Sizes can be adapted within a little if necessary.

THE entrance gate shown is a wooden one, replacing one of iron with adjacent railings which were removed during the war. In numerous cases this has been necessary, and in this instance the low wall (about 3 ft.) provided for a gate and trellis arrangement which could be erected at a moderate cost. Western red cedar was the timber used, but, if a prime timber such as oak is out of the question, sound Baltic red deal or well-seasoned larch may be used.

The Gate.—5 ft. 6 ins. high by 3 ft. wide, has these parts :—

(A) 2 Stiles, 5 ft. 4½ ins. by 4½ ins. by 1⅝ ins. thick.

(B) 1 Top Rail, 3 ft. by 6 ins. by 1⅞ ins. thick. At ends this curves to 4½ ins.

(C) 2 Rails, 3 ft. by 4½ ins. by 1¼ ins. thick.

(D) 5 Bars, 5 ft. by 2¼ ins. by ¾ in. thick.

Note that top rail (B), of the same thickness as stiles, is tenoned right through. It may be wedged with two wedges. The two lower rails (C) have bareface tenons (Fig. 2). They stand in ¾ in. so that the upright bars (D) may be nailed to them in alignment with stiles. At top these bars are tongued to rail (B) ; at bottom they finish with a slight bevel.

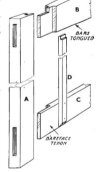

FIG. 2. JOINT DETAILS.

A brace is hardly necessary, but if it is preferred to add this, as per dotted line in Fig. 3, the length will be 3 ft. 6 ins., from 2¾ ins. by 1½ ins. stuff. The brace, of course, springs from the hanging side and is notched in at both ends.

Posts, 6 ins. square, may stand 6 ft. from ground, but in length an extra 2 ft. must be allowed for sinking.

Trellis.—Should this be added the height may appropriately be that of the gate stiles. It is intended that the trellis should be fitted independently behind the wall—that is, if the posts, in relation to thickness of wall, permit of this. The lath stuff might be of 2 ins. by ⅜ in. if the spacings are not less than 4 ins. between uprights. These latter will be carried down to within 12 ins. or 15 ins. from ground, being supported at intervals of about 6 ft. by 4 ins. by 4 ins. posts. A fillet connects the trellis to gate posts.

Should a smaller gate of the same type be required, suitable dimensions are : for a width of 2 ft. 9 ins., fix height at 5 ft. 2 ins. ; for a width of 2 ft. 6 ins., fix height at 4 ft. 7½ ins. Detail parts will be proportionately lighter.

Keep the gate well painted unless it is in western red cedar which needs no preservative. Pay special attention to the end grain which is the most vulnerable part.

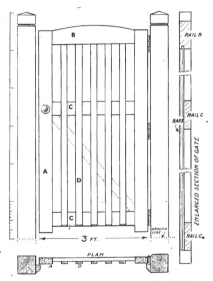

FIG. 3. ELEVATION AND PLAN, AND ENLARGED SECTION.

40

LIGHT GARDEN ARMCHAIR

AS the timber required for this type of outdoor armchair is not excessive, straight-grained plain oak should be the first choice. Birch or beech is a suitable alternative. The parts required are these :—

		ft. ins.	ins.	ins.
(A)	4 Legs	2 1	2	1⅜
(B)	2 End rails	1 6	2	1⅜
(C)	2 Side seat rails	1 9½	2	1⅜
(D)	2 Seart ails (front and back)	1 10½	2	⅞
(E)	2 Stretchers	1 10	2	⅞
(F)	2 Back uprights	2 1	2	1⅜
(G)	Back rail	1 10½	4	⅞
(H)	do.	1 10½	2	⅞
(J)	2 Arms	1 3½	2½	⅞
(K)	2 Seat laths	2 0	4¼	⅞
	4 do.	2 0	2¾	⅞

Lengths allow for joints and fitting, but thicknesses are net. The legs, etc., are given a thickness of 1⅜ ins., but this might be reduced to 1¼ ins. if in oak.

Construction of Frame.—The triangular ends are first prepared, the legs (A) standing 20 ins. apart. The top joint is a mitred bridle, and a stub tenon (X, Fig. 4) is cut to enter the arm (J). The end rails (B) are through-tenoned to the legs, all joints being of course fixed by painting and then pinned with hardwood pegs.

The seat height is 15 ins., this allowing for a cushion. At Fig. 3 the seat is shown level, but if thought desirable it could have a slope of about ½ in. towards the back. Bearing these two points in mind, mark carefully for the half-lap joints on legs and side seat rails (C). Note particularly that the rails are not exactly centred, the projection at back being about an inch more than at front (Fig. 3). By laying the rails across the completed leg ends the bevels may be accurately marked.

Before fitting the rails (C) prepare the front and back seat rails (D) and also the stretchers (E). It will be seen that the rails (C and D) form a seat frame, the corners of which are through-dovetailed. The two stretchers are dovetail-notched to the end rails (B). Assemble by fitting the legs to the side rails (C) by means of the halved joints, painting and pinning as before. Test the whole for squareness.

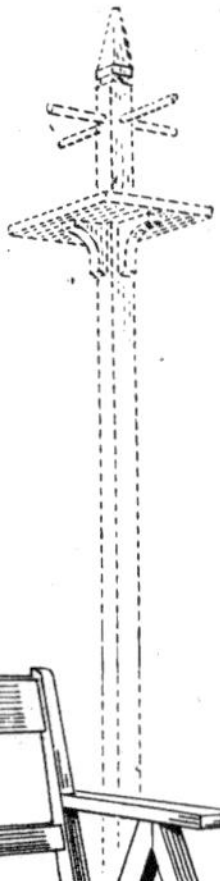

Back, Arms, and Seat.—The back supports (F) are tapered from 2 ins. to 1¼ ins. at top. The thickness of 1⅜ ins. may be retained throughout ; or, if preferred, a taper to 1⅛ ins. may be worked. The supports are through-mortised for the back rails (G and H) and half-lapped to engage the side seat rails (C). To the legs they are notched, as shown, and pinned. Dotted lines at Fig. 3 will show the rake of back. The back rails (G and H) are through-tenoned.

Arms (J), tenoned to back supports, taper from 2½ ins. at front to 2 ins. at back. They may be mortised for a stub tenon on legs, or may be held by driving in a hardwood peg aslant, as at Z, Fig 4. As chairs are apt to be lifted by the *arms* it may be found wise to screw a pair of small angle iron plates underneath (see X).

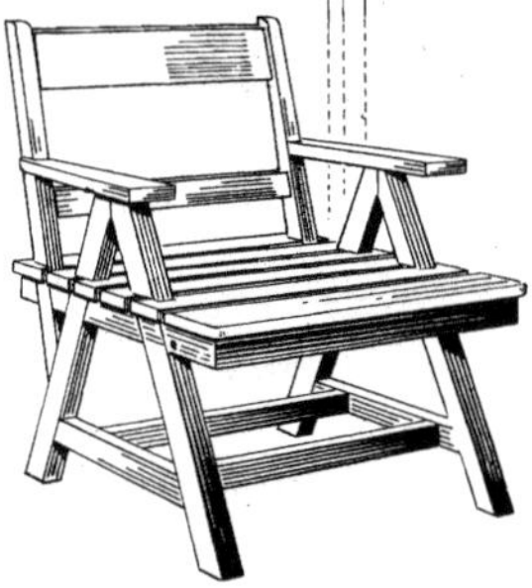

GARDEN ARMCHAIR.

The seat laths (K) are screwed with round-head brass screws driven in flush. Note that the front and back laths are wider than the intermediate ones, the latter being arranged so that they will neatly clear the legs. Laths overhang the seat rails (C) by ¾ in.

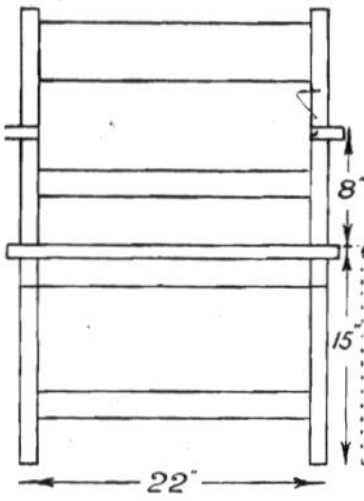

FIG. 2. SCALE ELEVATION.

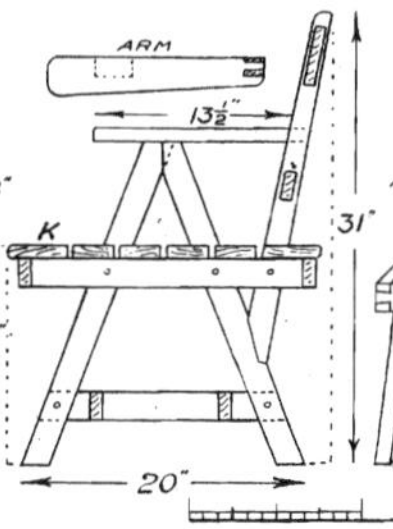

FIG. 3. END SECTIONAL VIEW.

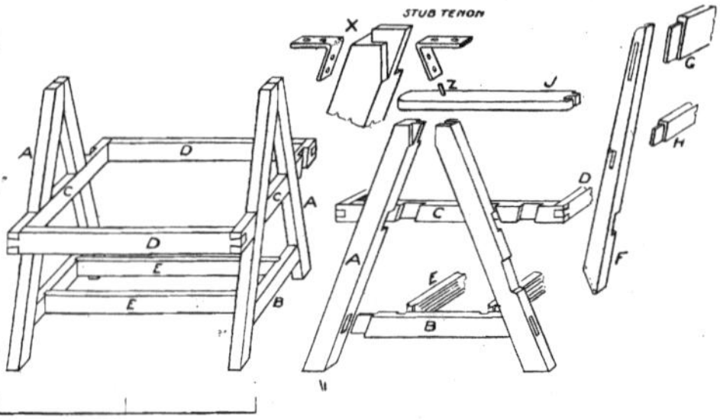

FIG. 4. SHOWING THE ASSEMBLY OF PARTS.

TOOL SHED
FOR THE ALLOTMENT

FIG. I. **FOR EVERY KEEN GARDENER.**
The suggested size of 4 ft. **square** and height of 7 ft. at door can be adapted within a little if desired. **If wood is not available the sides can be covered with asbestos board or galvanised iron.**

WHEREVER a garden or allotment is cultivated a tool shed is an absolute necessity. In the majority of cases it is impossible to find room within the dwelling-house to store the necessary tools and appliances required in the cultivation of the home-garden, as, in addition to forks, spades, and such-like tools, a lawn mower, and perhaps a small roller have to be accommodated. Similarly, when an allotment is being cultivated there is no task so irksome as having to carry the tools forward and back. Even more than in the home-garden, a shelter from an occasional storm, and a seat on which to rest is very desirable.

The tool shed, shown in Fig. 1, and described here is suitable for the garden or the allotment, and, although sizes are suggested, those for width and depth may be adapted to meet individual needs. For the home-garden some care should be taken with the selection of material, and the workmanship, so that the shed may conform with its surroundings. Wood must, of course, be used for the framework. Matched or weather boarding, if obtainable, may be used for covering, but asbestos cement sheets make a good substitute, while corrugated sheets could be used for covering the roof.

For the allotment a wood-framed shed, covered even with galvanised iron, answers the purpose quite well. It is advisable to fit a small window in the back of the shed, and it will be beneficial to the garden and its crops if means are taken to collect the rain-water draining from the roof of the shed.

Framework.—Stuff not less than 2 ins. square should be used for framing. In the two ends (Fig. 2) the front and back uprights are half-lapped and screwed to the top and bottom rails, as shown in Fig. 3, and the middle upright is notched in and nailed, as shown in Fig. 4, while two braces are fitted to stiffen the framing. Shaped bracket pieces could be fitted between the front uprights and the projecting ends of the top rails to strengthen the framing. These are set out to a radius of about 1 ft. 6 ins., and are nailed in place.

In the back (Fig. 5) the end uprights are half-lapped and screwed to the top and bottom rails, the middle rail is notched in and nailed, as are the uprights forming the window opening and the lower middle upright. A couple of braces are again fitted to stiffen the framework. In the front (Fig. 6) the end uprights are half-lapped and screwed to the top and bottom rails, and the inner uprights forming the doorway are notched in and nailed, while a couple of short rails should be fitted on each side between the end and inner uprights.

Foundation.—Before erecting the framework it will be advisable, especially in the home-garden, to level the site and lay a concrete foundation for the shed, and make provision for fixing it down by bedding in bolts. The front and back frames fit within the two end frames, as shown in Fig. 7, the sections being fixed together with bolts passing through the uprights.

Roof.—The roof framework is arranged by fixing three purlins across the top rails of the end frames, as shown in Fig. 7. The purlins should overhang a few inches, and short blocks are fitted above the top rails of the end frames in front and behind the front and back purlins, the ends of the rails and blocks being trimmed to the perpendicular line. A fascia board about 4 ins. deep is fixed across the back edge of the roof. It is nailed to the ends of the top rails of the two end sections, and to the blocks fixed above them, while its top edge is cleaned off level with the top of the blocks to allow the roof covering to fit above and overhang slightly at the back, as shown in Fig. 8. The ends of this board should extend about 2 ins. beyond the ends of the purlins at each side.

The roof covering should be fitted in place at this stage, and work on the roof is carried forward by fitting a front fascia board and two end barge boards. All should be deep enough to finish level with the top of the roof covering. The front fascia board is 2 ins. longer at each end than the purlins, and its bottom edge may be shaped, as shown. Grooves about ¼ in. deep are cut in both the front and back fascia boards in line with the ends of the purlins. The front fascia board is nailed to the front ends of the top rails of the end sections and the blocks above, while the barge boards fit in the grooves in both the front and back fascia boards, and are nailed to the ends of the purlins.

When the roof covering has been finally fixed down, wood capping pieces should be fitted above the front fascia board and the barge boards, the cappings being wide enough to overhang the roof covering and have weather grooves cut in the underside, as shown in Fig. 9, the end cappings being mitred into the front capping, as shown in Fig. 10.

Side Coverings.—If the sides are covered with boards the work will be quite straightforward, but if it is decided to use asbestos cement sheets it will be as well to obtain the sizes available beforehand and arrange the size of the shed accordingly. The sheets are fixed by nailing to the middle uprights, and by nailing fillets around the edges. Much information on fixing both flat sheets for the sides, and corrugated sheets for the roof is given in the October, 1945, WOODWORKER MAGAZINE.

If the sides are boarded, the boards will of course be brought up tight under the roof covering, but if asbestos cement sheets are used the top fillets will have to be somewhat wider than the others to cover the openings at the top where the purlins rise above the front, back, and end framework, as shown in Fig. 8.

Window.—The window in the back could be fixed or made to open as desired. If it is made to open it will be necessary to fit a bevelled sill across the bottom of the window opening. The sash could be of 1¼ in. stuff with the stiles and top rail 2 ins. wide and the bottom rail 3 ins. All the members are rebated for the glass on the outside, and moulded or chamfered inside, while mortise and tenon joints are used for framing.

Door.—The door will be best made from grooved and tongued boards, battened and braced. It may be hung at either side as is most convenient, and should, of course, be fitted with a lock and key. A seat may be easily arranged inside the shed by fixing two battens across the end framework, as suggested by the dotted lines in Fig. 2, and resting a seat board above them. It may be found convenient to have the seat board loose as it may then be moved if it is desired to store anything bulky inside the shed.

Guttering.—An ordinary cast iron rain-water gutter could be fitted at the back of the shed to catch the rain-water, or one may be easily improvised in wood and may give the best results. It is shown fitted to the shed in Fig. 11, with a large oil or tar drum to hold the water. The gutter is made from ⅞ in. stuff with two sides long enough to reach from end to end of the roof. One side is 3½ ins. deep at the outlet and the other 3 ins., the first tapering up to 3 ins. and the other 2½ ins. deep at the ends to allow the water to flow readily. Pieces 3 ins. wide and of a convenient length to form the sides of the outlet are half-lapped and screwed to the sides, as shown in Figs. 12 and 13, while the bottoms, ends of the outlet and the end stops are nailed between. It will be advisable to paint, or treat with white lead, all the joints in the gutter, and it is fixed with the wide side in, through which screws are driven for fixing.

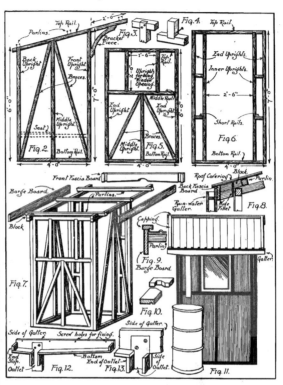

FIGS. 2-12. MAIN SIZES, FRAMES, ASSEMBLY, JOINTS, AND DETAILS.

GARDEN BOOT SCRAPER

BOOT SCRAPER FOR THE GARDEN.
(Post shown sunk in ground.)

It is a good plan to have several boot scrapers about the garden, especially where the soil is of clay. All that you require are two lengths of 2 ins. by 2 ins. hardwood about 18 ins. long. Slightly pare the bottom ends and then tar them for about 12 ins. of their length. This portion is sunk in the ground and a few stones rammed round the posts to keep it firm. The distance between the posts can be 12 ins. and at a height of 4 ins. to 5 ins. from ground the scraper should be attached. If a large " D " file happens to be available and of no further use, it will answer as a scraper admirably, both tang and end being fixed to the post by means of stout galvanised staples hammered well home.

43

JOINTS FOR GARDEN CARPENTRY

THEIR APPLICATION

MANY of the simpler joints are particularly applicable to outdoor work such as garden tool sheds, wicket gates, rustic fencing, and rustic garden seats.

Shed Joints.—Fig. 1 shows a diagram of the wooden gable end of a simple shed where all mortising and tenoning has been eliminated. It can be made of 3 ins. by 2 ins. clean white deal, and all the halving joints would be simply smeared with thick white paint which has been slightly run down with an oil varnish. The joints should be screwed together. The enlarged details of such a shed end (also with edge view) is sketched in Fig. 3. Suitable preparation for seating the ridge is shown in Fig. 2, and it will be noticed that the tie piece (F) is nailed across the blades on the inside of the framework. In Fig. 4, a sketch is given which shows most of the joints separated. The piece (E) may be either tenoned at one end and half-lapped at the other end, or it may be half-lapped at each end as suggested in Fig. 3.

Medium-sized sheds are usually made up out of six separate frames : two end frames, two side frames, and two roof frames. In Fig. 5 is shown the method of fixing the end frames to the side frames. In this sketch we show both the end and the side frames with haunched tenon joints ; workers who experience difficulty in tackling these can resort to the halving joint. In Fig. 5 (C) is shown a coach-screw, which, fitted with a suitable washer under its head, provides a sound method of fastening timbers together, allowing (as it does) a job to be readily taken apart. When using a coachscrew, bore through the first piece of timber, the diameter of the hole being that of the neck of the screw. The fit should be easy so that the screw

can be turned around in the hole with the fingers. In the second piece of timber the hole should equal the diameter of the lower part of the screw, minus its thread. If this procedure is followed and the threaded portion be daubed with a little tallow, the screw will draw all tight without any risk of splitting the wood. At Fig. 6 is given the method adopted by some makers who supply ready-made sheds at low prices. In this case the mortising and tenoning is set out and proceeded with in the usual manner, after which the upright post is sawn in two diagonally. This means that, instead of two pieces being required at each corner of the shed (as at Fig. 5), there is a saving of one piece of wood at each corner of the shed. If the upright pieces are 3 ins. by 3 ins., as at Fig. 6, they will stand such a diagonal cut and the job will be quite firm when screwed together again. If you anticipate any difficulty in sawing the wood diagonally, after you have tenoned it, simply take the four pieces down to your local saw mill, where they will "cant" their guide fence on the circular sawing machine and cut the four pieces in less than five minutes. This method will give you a perfect fit without having to plane the edges. We do not recommend this diagonal cut with timber less than 3 ins. by 3 ins. ; a halving joint at the corners is not suitable for this method of construction.

Gates.—The construction of a simple wicket or garden gate is shown at Fig. 7. Here we have the barefaced tenon joint. This joint is shouldered on one side only and the difference in thickness between the uprights and the cross rails is equal to the thickness of the upright laths, which eventually leaves the work flush on its face side. If laths are not desired it is quite easy to fill up the interior of the gate with ⅝ in. or ¾ in. tongued, grooved, and vee'd match-

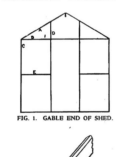

FIG. 1. GABLE END OF SHED.

FIG. 2. THE SHED RIDGE.

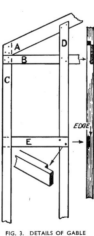

FIG. 3. DETAILS OF GABLE END OF SHED.

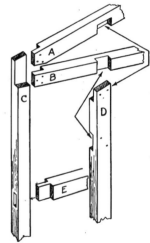

FIG. 4. THE FRAME JOINTS.

USE PAINT WHEN ASSEMBLING OUTDOOR WOODWORK JOINTS

boarding. Cheap but clean slate battens may be used for the laths.

The uprights or stiles should be out of 3 ins. by 2 ins. white or red deal ; or, if the pocket permits, they are best made out of oak. Slate battens measuring approximately 2 ins. by ¾ in. can normally be obtained at a builder's yard.

Fencing Joint.—The method of jointing the cross rails into the uprights by a diagonal cut for the bit of fencing at the bottom of a vegetable plot is given at Fig. 8. Simply cut the ends of the cross rails on the bevel so that they fit each other ; then smear them with thick paint or creosote and drive them into the mortise, securing them with a couple of nails.

Rustic Work Joints.—For rough fencing which is to be made out of branches, etc., use a similar method of jointing which is shown in Fig. 9. Tenoning rustic work into the uprights is shown in Fig. 10. The curved shoulders of the tenon may be cut away with the bow-saw.

A rustic lap joint secured with wrought nails is given in Fig. 11. This may easily be formed with the aid of a saw and chisel. The right-angled notch joint in Fig. 12 may be treated in a similar manner.

In Fig. 13 the upright post has a dowel formed upon it, and the two portions of the halving joint are bored to receive the dowel. If preferred, a square stub-tenon

could be used. If the dowel is used a coarse rasp may be used to give it the cylindrical formation. In the same figure the method of notching and nailing the small corner strut is suggested.

Wrought or cut nails hold better than the round bright nails in most timbers, but in any case suitable holes should be bored in the first piece of wood as a preventative against splitting the ends.

Rustic joints do not call for the finish that is so desirable on better class carpentry, but the worker should remember either to creosote or paint-daub all the internal parts of the joints when they are assembled; otherwise the rain will soak into the nicks and quickly set up decay. It is a good plan to have at hand a flat tin tobacco box filled with tallow so that the point of each nail may be dipped into the tallow before it is driven home. This idea makes for easy driving.

FIG. 9. JOINT FOR ROUGH RUSTIC FENCE.

FIG. 10. TENONED RUSTIC JOINT.

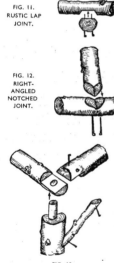

FIG. 11. RUSTIC LAP JOINT.

FIG. 12. RIGHT-ANGLED NOTCHED JOINT.

FIG. 13. UPRIGHT POST WITH DOWEL. ALSO SHOWING METHOD OF NOTCHING AND NAILING CORNER STRUT.

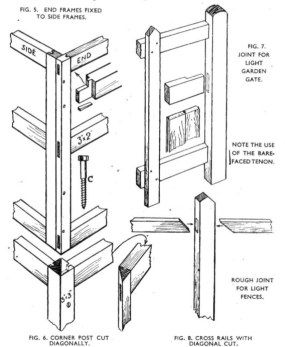

FIG. 5. END FRAMES FIXED TO SIDE FRAMES.

SIDE

END

3"×2"

C

3"×3"

FIG. 7. JOINT FOR LIGHT GARDEN GATE.

NOTE THE USE OF THE BARE-FACED TENON.

ROUGH JOINT FOR LIGHT FENCES.

FIG. 6. CORNER POST CUT DIAGONALLY.

FIG. 8. CROSS RAILS WITH DIAGONAL CUT.

Printed in Great Britain
by Amazon